THE EPISTLE TO THE EPHESIANS

THE EPISTLE TO
THE EPHESIANS

A Verse-by-Verse Exposition

BY

F. F. BRUCE

M.A.(Cantab.), D.D.(Aberd.).

FLEMING H. REVELL COMPANY
OLD TAPPAN, NEW JERSEY

This edition is issued by
special arrangement with
PICKERING & INGLIS LTD.
the British publishers

First published 1961
Reprinted   1968
   ,,   1970
   ,,   1973
   ,,   1974

Printed in the United States of America

TO

SPENCER AND BERTHA THOMAS

PREFACE

THIS exposition of the Epistle to the Ephesians was originally undertaken for the periodical *Knowing the Scriptures*. When about half of it had appeared there, publication of that periodical was discontinued. The part which had already appeared was then reprinted in several successive issues of *The Believer's Magazine*, which also published the remainder of the work. For this kindness I am very grateful to Mr. Andrew Borland, M.A., Editor of *The Believer's Magazine*. I am further indebted to him and to the publishers of both the periodicals mentioned, Messrs. John Ritchie, Ltd., for granting me their ready permission to have the work reproduced, with slight revisions and expansions, in book form.

The exposition is intended for the general Christian reader who is interested in serious Bible study, not for the professional or specialist student. Textual, linguistic and other critical questions have therefore been touched upon lightly; the main aim has been to bring out the meaning and message of the Epistle.

The Bible text used throughout, except where otherwise indicated, is the Revised Version of 1881. This remains, in spite of many more recent translations (including the New English Bible of 1961) the most helpful English version of the New Testament for purposes of accurate study.   F.F.B.

March, 1961

CONTENTS

PART I

THE NEW COMMUNITY IN THE PURPOSE OF GOD

PART II

THE NEW COMMUNITY IN THE LIFE OF BELIEVERS

INTRODUCTION

I. AUTHORSHIP

THE Epistle to the Ephesians introduces itself, as do the other Pauline letters, with the name of Paul—'Paul, an apostle of Christ Jesus through the will of God'. At the beginning of the third chapter the writer refers to himself again as Paul. This might well seem to settle the question of authorship decisively, the more so as the vocabulary and thought of the epistle are so thoroughly Pauline. It has, however, been urged repeatedly in more recent years that the Epistle to the Ephesians was composed at the time when the first collection of Paul's letters was published, in order to serve as a suitable introduction to the published collection. The writer, presumably one of Paul's disciples, endeavoured to give an exposition of Paul's central teaching and to convey it as far as possible in language borrowed from Paul's own writings.[1]

If the Epistle to the Ephesians was not written directly by Paul, but by one of his disciples in the apostle's name, then its author was the greatest Paulinist of all time—a disciple who assimilated his master's thought more thoroughly than anyone else ever did. The man who could write Ephesians must have been the apostle's equal, if not his superior, in mental stature and spiritual insight. For Ephesians is a distinctive work with its own unity of theme. If we study it word by word and phrase by phrase, it may look like a compilation from the other Pauline epistles; but when we stand back and view it as a whole, it has an individuality and a message of its own. It was no mean judge of literary excellence, Samuel Taylor Coleridge, who described Ephesians as 'the divinest composition of man'.[2] Not only is it 'the quintessence of Paulinism';[3] it carries Paul's teaching forward

---

[1] See, for example, E. J. Goodspeed, *The Meaning of Ephesians* (Chicago, 1933) and *The Key to Ephesians* (1956). A more technical study, leading to similar conclusions, is C. L. Mitton, *The Epistle to the Ephesians* (Oxford, 1951).

[2] *Table Talk.*

[3] *The Quintessence of Paulinism* is the title of an important study of Paul's theology by A. S. Peake, first published in the *Bulletin of the John Rylands Library*, 4 (1917-18), pp. 285-311.

to a more advanced stage of revelation and application than that represented by the earlier epistles. The author, if he was not Paul himself, has carried the apostle's thinking to its logical conclusion, beyond the point where the apostle stopped, and has placed the coping-stone on the massive structure of Paul's teaching. Of such a second Paul early Christian history has no knowledge.

II. TIME AND PLACE OF WRITING

That Paul was a prisoner at the time of writing is expressly stated more than once in the course of the letter. He refers to himself as 'I Paul, the prisoner of Christ Jesus in behalf of you Gentiles' (3. 1), as 'the prisoner in the Lord' (4. 1), and as 'an ambassador in chains' (6. 20). We have the evidence of Acts for two periods of imprisonment which Paul underwent, each of two years' duration, one in Caesarea (24. 27) and the other in Rome (28. 30). The single night's imprisonment in Philippi (Acts 16. 23 ff.) naturally does not enter into the reckoning here. But before either of his more lengthy experiences of imprisonment recorded in Acts he could speak of himself as having been 'in prisons more abundantly' than any other apostle (2 Cor. 11. 23). Of these more abundant imprisonments there is good reason to believe that one at least must be dated during his Ephesian ministry.[1] The time and place of the present imprisonment does not make much difference to the exposition of Ephesians. But the position adopted here is the common one, that Ephesians (as also Colossians and Philemon)[2] was written at some point during Paul's Roman imprisonment, between the beginning of A.D. 60 and the end of A.D. 61. If any orderly progress at all is to be traced in Paul's thinking, then Ephesians must be dated last of all his letters to churches, and immediately after Colossians.

---

[1] On this subject see G. S. Duncan, *St. Paul's Ephesian Ministry* (London, 1929).
[2] Philippians is commonly reckoned along with these three, as one of the four 'Captivity Epistles', but these three stand in a group by themselves.

III. The Recipients

A comparison of Eph. 6. 21 f. with Col. 4. 7 f. makes it evident that Ephesians was sent to its destination by the hand of Tychicus at the same time as Colossians. We may therefore look for the destination of both letters in the same area. Colossians was manifestly sent to the church at Colossae, in the Phrygian region of the province of Asia. The words 'at Ephesus' in Eph. 1. 1 might seem to put the destination of this letter beyond question, were it not for the fact that some of our earliest and weightiest authorities for the text omit these two words. It would be surprising, too, to have such an absence of personal references in a letter written by Paul to a church in whose midst he had spent the best part of three years. The most acceptable view, having regard to the general character of the letter, is that it was intended for all the churches of the province of Asia, some of which were personally known to Paul, while others were not (cf. Col. 2. 1). While the message of the letter was never intended to be limited to one local church only, we may quite justifiably call it 'The Epistle to the Ephesians', provided that we remember that it was sent also to other churches in the province of which Ephesus was the capital city.

IV. Occasion and Theme

For nearly three years—probably from the summer of A.D. 52 to the spring of A.D. 55—Paul had established his headquarters in Ephesus, the chief city of the Roman province of Asia, and not only planted a strong church in that city, but with the help of a number of colleagues evangelized the whole province. No doubt all the seven churches of Asia mentioned in Revelation, and others as well, traced their origin to these years (Acts 19. 8-10).

During the following years Paul kept in close touch with the churches of Asia, and some of their members came to see him while he was a prisoner in Rome. One of these visitors was Epaphras, Paul's colleague who had evangelized the area of the province of Asia watered by the River Lycus, and helped to found the churches of Colossae, Laodicea and Hierapolis. He brought Paul news of a form of false teaching which was attracting many of the Christians in those churches, especially in the church of Colossae. This was a theosophical amalgam of Jewish and pagan elements ,which made much of the hierarchies of principalities and powers in the universe. It was hospitable enough to make some room for Christ in its scheme of things, but its whole tendency was to deny His supremacy and the completeness of His redemptive work. To counter this unhealthy influence Paul wrote a letter to the Colossian church and sent it by the hand of his friend Tychicus, a native of the province of Asia, who had also been paying him a visit and was now on his way home again.

As Paul considered his reply to the Colossian heresy, he was led on to develop the theme of Christ's person and work in relation to the whole universe, including those principalities and powers which played so dominant a part in that heresy. Christ had shown Himself superior to those powers first because they owed their existence to Him, and then because they were ignominiously routed by Him when they assailed Him on the cross. This cosmic significance of the person and work of Christ was no. new idea to Paul: already he proclaimed 'one Lord, Jesus Christ, through whom are all things, and we through him' (1 Cor. 8. 6), and taught that the liberation which Christ had effected by His death would one day be enjoyed by the whole creation (Rom. 8. 19-22). But what is hinted at here and there in some of his earlier letters is elaborated in the Epistle to the Colossians, where Christ is portrayed as the One through whom all the powers in the universe were created and the One who by His triumphant death has brought them all into captivity to Himself. Moreover, His people are so vitally united to Him, being members of the body of which He is the head, that they share in His triumph and have no need to pay homage to those elemental forces which formerly held them in bondage.

But if the Church is the body of the exalted Christ, what is her relation to His cosmic rôle? What is her relation to the universe over which He is enthroned as Lord, and to God's eternal purpose? These questions were not dealt with in the Epistle to the Colossians, but they continued to exercise the apostle's mind after he had put his signature to that epistle, until he was gripped by the vision which he sets before us in Ephesians, and began to dictate the contents of this further letter, not in the swift, argumentative style with which we are so familiar from other letters of his, but in an inspired mood of meditative adoration and prayer. It was then sent, also by the hand of Tychicus, to the churches of the province of Asia to serve in some sort as his testament[1] to dearly-loved friends whom, so far as he knew, he might never see again,[2] as well as to others whom he had never yet seen.[3]

This view of the origin and conception of the Epistle to the Ephesians—the view taken in the following exposition—is the most satisfactory explanation of the remarkably close affinity which exists between it and the Epistle to the Colossians.

In many Protestant circles it has been customary to look upon the doctrine of justification by faith as the be-all and end-all of Paul's teaching. Justification by faith is certainly fundamental to all his thinking, and it comes readily to the surface no matter what subject he is dealing with. Even in Ephesians it is uncompromisingly affirmed: 'by grace have ye been saved through faith; and that not of yourselves: it is the gift of God: not of works, that no man should glory' (Eph. 2. 8 f.). It was inevitable and salutary in the Reformation age that the attention of Christians should be directed afresh to the ground on which men and women are accepted as righteous by God. But it is a pity when Paulinism is identified so exclusively with the emphasis of Galatians and Romans that the corporate and cosmic insights of Colossians and Ephesians are overlooked, or felt to be un-Pauline. True Paulinism has room for both, and our Christian thinking must similarly make room for both if it is not to become lop-sided and defective.

---

[1] Cf. J. N. Sanders in *Studies in Ephesians*, ed. F. L. Cross (London, 1956), p. 16.
[2] See Acts 20. 25, 38.
[3] See Col. 2. 1.

In Ephesians the Church, the body of Christ, is a new community created by God to be the dwelling-place and vehicle of His Spirit, with a view to the consummation of His eternal purpose and the establishment of His dominion throughout all creation. As Paul puts it elsewhere, creation at present is frustrated and in bondage to futility and decay, but one day it is to be emancipated from this bondage to share 'the liberty of the glory of the children of God' (Rom. 8. 21). But nowhere is this glorious purpose unfolded so fully and clearly as in the Epistle to the Ephesians. 'This Epistle', says a great Scottish-American theologian, Dr. John A. Mackay, 'because of the nature of the problem with which it deals, is the most modern of the New Testament writings'.[1] Then he begs his readers' pardon for introducing 'a lyrical note', which is well worthy of quotation:

> I can never forget that the reading of this Pauline letter, when I was a boy in my teens, exercised a more decisive influence upon my thought and imagination than was ever wrought upon me before or since by the perusal of any piece of literature. The romance of the part played by Jesus Christ in making my personal salvation possible and in mediating God's cosmic plan so set my spirit aflame that I laid aside in an ecstasy of delight Dumas' *Count of Monte Cristo*, which I happened to be reading at the time. That was my encounter with the Cosmic Christ. The Christ who was and is became the passion of my life. I have to admit, without shame or reserve, that, as a result of that encounter, I have been unable to think of my own life or the life of mankind or the life of the cosmos apart from Jesus Christ. He came to me and challenged me in the writings of St. Paul. I responded. The years that have followed have been but a footnote to that encounter.[2]

Paul has already stated in Colossians that God's purpose is through Christ 'to reconcile all things unto himself, having made peace through the blood of his cross; through him, I say, whether things upon the earth, or things in the heavens' (Col. 1. 20). In Ephesians this theme of reconciliation is carried farther. God's purpose is 'to sum up all things in Christ, the things in the heavens, and the things upon the earth' (Eph. 1. 10)—in other words, to bring all creation to the point where it finds its true

---

[1] *A Preface to Christian Theology* (London, 1942), p. 96.
[2] *Op. cit.*, p. 97.

head in Christ. In this purpose of cosmic reconciliation the Church has an essential part to play, for the Church is herself God's masterpiece of reconciliation. Not only is it composed of men and women who have individually been reconciled to God through Christ; it is composed of men and women who have also been reconciled to one another through Christ. In particular —and Paul never got over the wonder of this—the Church comprised both Jews and Gentiles. In this new fellowship the cleavage between these two mutually exclusive divisions of mankind had disappeared; Christ had reconciled them both 'in one body unto God through the cross, having slain the enmity thereby' (Eph. 2. 16), and had in Himself recreated Jews and Gentiles alike as 'one new man, so making peace' (Eph. 2. 15). Christ had broken down the barrier which kept Jew and Gentile apart, and brought them together as fellow-members of His one body.

Perhaps the cleavage between Jew and Gentile does not seem so terribly important to us. It was of prime importance to a man of Paul's birth and training—and the emphasis laid upon it in this epistle may be accounted an incidental token of Pauline authorship. But we can think of many other cleavages in the world of today, more recalcitrant and malignant than the cleavage between Jew and Gentile now is—cleavages of nation, race, colour, class, religion and culture which engender bitter hostility and threaten our world with annihilation unless they are removed. But how can this be done? The message of the Epistle to the Ephesians is that only through Christ, in the fellowship of His body, can iron curtains, colour-bars, class-warfare and all other divisions of this kind be brought to an end. In His new community 'there cannot be Greek and Jew, circumcision and uncircumcision, barbarian, Scythian, bondman, freeman: but Christ is all, and in all' (Col. 3. 11). It is only Christ our peace who can bring together the people on either side of these barricades, by first bringing them to Himself, thus making them one with Him and therefore with one another. In this reconciling work of His the Church has a service to perform, not only as God's masterpiece of reconciliation, but also as His instrument for bringing about

2

the cosmic reconciliation which is His ultimate purpose. But the Church as she is in the eyes of men must conform to the Church as she is in the purpose of God, if she is to be an effective instrument to this end. Only as the Church is seen to be the community of the reconciled can she convincingly proclaim the gospel of reconciliation to others. If the same cleavages of class and race and colour as we see in the world are tolerated in the Church, her witness is nullified; the salt of the earth has lost its taste and has become good for nothing. That this is a necessary and humbling reflection today needs no emphasizing.

For this reason Paul adds to his portrayal of the Church in the purpose of God practical injunctions to ensure that this purpose may not be hindered by the daily life of Christians on earth. This second part of the epistle, which begins with the fourth chapter, is linked to the foregoing part by the particle 'therefore' (4. 1); the practical injunctions are the logical outcome of the truth revealed in the first three chapters.

V. EARLY USE AND RECOGNITION

A date of A.D. 60 or shortly after has been suggested above for the Epistle.

There is good evidence that Paul's epistles, which had been treasured in the various places to which they were severally sent, began to be gathered together and thereafter to circulate as a collection about the end of the first century A.D. Clement of Rome, writing about A.D. 95, shows his acquaintance with a number of Paul's letters, and Ephesians is possibly to be reckoned among them. Ephesians was certainly known to Ignatius of Antioch before his martyrdom about A.D. 115, to his junior contemporary and fellow-bishop, Polycarp of Smyrna, who wrote his one surviving epistle soon after Ignatius's martyrdom, and to the authors of the *Epistle of Barnabas* and the *Shepherd of Hermas*, which also belong to the earlier years of the second century. The heresiarch Marcion, who published his 'canon' or list of authoritative Christian books at Rome about 144, included Ephesians among the ten Pauline epistles contained in that list; he entitled it, however, the 'Epistle to the Laodiceans' (probably identifying it with the letter referred to by Paul in Col. 4. 16). Later in the second century Irenaeus of Lyons, Clement of Alexandria, Tertullian of Carthage, and the Muratorian list of canonical books, drawn up at Rome, attest the unanimity with which the Christian world accepted the apostolic authorship and canonicity of Ephesians.

Indeed, if we go back to the New Testament age, signs are not lacking in the Pastoral Epistles (those to Timothy and Titus) and in 1 Peter which suggest that Ephesians was known and used in the writing of these letters.

VI. FOR FURTHER STUDY

Of all helps to the study of this Epistle I am chiefly indebted to *St. Paul's Epistle to the Ephesians: A Revised Text and Translation with Exposition and Notes*, by J. Armitage Robinson (London: Macmillan, 1904). This includes an exposition of the English text and exegesis of the Greek text.

B. F. Westcott left an incomplete work on the Epistle which was edited after his death by J. M. Schulhof and published under the title *St. Paul's Epistle to the Ephesians: The Greek Text with Notes and Addenda* (London: Macmillan, 1906). Notes on the Greek text of the first fourteen verses are included in another posthumous volume: *Notes on the Epistles of St. Paul*, by J. B. Lightfoot (London: Macmillan, 1895). The other member of the great Cambridge trio, F. J. A. Hort, left an unfinished introduction to the Epistle which occupies the larger part of his *Prolegomena to St. Paul's Epistles to the Romans and the Ephesians* (London: Macmillan, 1895).

A few other studies, suitable for the Greekless reader, may be mentioned in chronological order. Charles Hodge's *Commentary on the Epistle to the Ephesians*, a careful theological exposition, first published in 1856, was reissued by the Wm. B. Eerdmans Publishing Co., Grand Rapids, Michigan, in 1950.[1]

---

[1] 'Most valuable', wrote C. H. Spurgeon of Hodge's commentary. 'With no writer do we more fully agree' (*Commenting and Commentaries*, p. 178).

Ephesian Studies, by H. C. G. Moule, described in the sub-title as 'Expository Readings on the Epistle of Saint Paul to the Ephesians' was first published in 1900 (London: Hodder & Stoughton); it has subsequently (1947) been reissued by Messrs. Pickering & Inglis, Ltd. (Bishop Moule had already contributed the volume on Ephesians to the Cambridge Bible in 1886.) The Moffatt version of Ephesians forms the basis for E. F. Scott's exposition of the Epistle in *The Epistles of Paul to the Colossians, to Philemon and to the Ephesians*, a volume in the Moffatt New Testament Commentary (London: Hodder & Stoughton, 1930). John A. Mackay, whose tribute to the influence of Ephesians has been quoted above, chose it as his theme when he was invited to deliver the Croall Lectures in New College, Edinburgh; his lectures were published under the title *God's Order: The Ephesian Letter and this Present Time* (New York: Macmillan; and London: Nisbet, 1953). William Barclay has given us a translation and exposition of *The Epistle to the Ephesians* in his inimitable Daily Bible Readings (Edinburgh: Church of Scotland Publications, 1956), reissued as part of the volume on *Letters to the Galatians and Ephesians* in The Daily Study Bible (Edinburgh: St. Andrew Press, 1958). An important symposium of *Studies in Ephesians* has been edited by F. L. Cross (London: Mowbray, 1956). E. K. Simpson contributed the commentary on Ephesians to the volume on *The Epistles of Paul to the Ephesians and to the Colossians* in the New International Commentary on the New Testament (Grand Rapids, Michigan: Eerdmans, 1957)[1]. The relevance of the Epistle to evangelism in the world of today is emphasized by Markus Barth in *The Broken Wall: A Study of the Epistle to the Ephesians* (London: Collins, 1960).

Several other works, dealing with various aspects and topics of the Epistle, are mentioned in the course of the introduction and exposition.

---

[1] Published in the United Kingdom as *The New London Commentary on the New Testament* (London: Marshall, Morgan & Scott).

VII. ANALYSIS OF THE EPISTLE

PART I

THE NEW COMMUNITY IN THE PURPOSE OF GOD (Chapters 1-3)

1. Salutation (1. 1-2).
2. A doxology (1. 3-14):
   amplified by the contemplation of—
   (a) the mystery of God's eternal purpose (1. 4-12);
   (b) the unity of Jew and Gentile in Christ (1. 13-14).
3. A prayer for wisdom (1. 15-2. 10):
   amplified by the description of God's power in—
   (a) the raising of Christ from the dead (1. 19-23);
   (b) the raising of those who were dead in sins (2. 1-10).
4. The Gentiles made heirs of the promises (2. 11-22).
5. The prayer for wisdom resumed (3. 1-13),
   with a digression on—
   (a) the mystery of Christ (3. 2-7);
   (b) Paul's stewardship of the mystery (3. 8-13).
6. The prayer for wisdom concluded (3. 14-19).
7. A doxology (3. 20-21).

PART II

THE NEW COMMUNITY IN THE LIFE OF BELIEVERS (Chapters 4-6)

1. Unity in diversity in the body of Christ (4. 1-16).
2. The old life and the new contrasted (4. 17-24).
3. Precepts of the new life (4. 25-5. 2).
4. Old darkness and new light (5. 3-21).
5. The Christian household (5. 22-6. 9):
   (a) Wives and husbands (5. 22-33);
   (b) Children and parents (6. 1-4);
   (c) Servants and masters (6. 5-9).
6. The panoply of God (6. 10-20).
7. Final greetings (6. 21-24).

PART I

THE NEW COMMUNITY IN THE PURPOSE OF GOD
(Chapters 1-3)

CHAPTER I

1. SALUTATION (1. 1-2)

V. 1 **Paul, an apostle of Christ Jesus through the will of God,**—Ancient letters regularly commenced with some such formula as 'X to Y, greeting'. Paul's letters are introduced by salutations based on this skeleton-formula, but the three elements in the formula (the sender's name, the addressees, and the greeting) are variously amplified in accordance with the circumstances. Paul's designation of himself here is identical with that in Col. 1. 1; the phrase 'through the will of God' in relation to his apostleship appears also in 1 Cor. 1. 1; 2 Cor. 1. 1; 2 Tim. 1. 1. The term 'apostle' (Gk. *apostolos*), as used of Christians in the New Testament has two meanings, a wider and a narrower. In the wider sense it is used of Christian missionaries in general (e.g. of Timothy and Silvanus in 1 Thess. 2. 6, or of Barnabas in Acts 14. 14), or of 'messengers of the churches' (as in 2 Cor. 8. 23).[1] But in the narrower sense, in which Paul uses it of himself here and elsewhere, it is confined to those who have received their commission directly and independently from Christ, apart from any mediation—that is to say, to Paul and to the Twelve.

to the saints which are at Ephesus, and the faithful in Christ Jesus:—The recipients of the letter are characterized by two terms frequently used of the followers of Christ in the New Testament; they are 'saints' or 'holy people' (Gk. *hagioi*), i.e. the people whom God has set apart for Himself, and they are 'faithful' or 'believers' (Gk. *pistoi*), i.e. those who have placed their wholehearted trust in Jesus as Son of God, Lord, and Saviour. The expression 'in Christ Jesus', however, does not denote Him as the One in whom they have believed so much as the One in whom they are brought together into a living fellowship. The solidarity of sin and death which members of the old creation have inherited 'in Adam' has given way to a solidarity of righteousness and life

---

[1] Cf. Epaphroditus, 'messenger' (R.V. margin 'apostle') of the Philippian church (Phil. 2. 25). Cf. Eph. 4. 11 with accompanying exposition (pp. 84 f.).

'in Christ Jesus' (or 'in Christ') for those who by faith have entered into the new creation.

The words 'at Ephesus' are omitted by papyrus 46[1] (the oldest authority for the text of the Pauline epistles), by the first hands in the Sinaitic and Vatican codices, and several other early witnesses. This omission is best explained by the view mentioned in the Introduction, that the epistle was intended not only for the Ephesian church but also for other churches of the province of Asia, and that some early copies had the name 'Ephesus' left out in order, possibly, that names of some other cities might be inserted in its place. The mention of some particular place here was no doubt intended from the beginning; it is most improbable that the recipients were addressed simply as 'the saints who are also faithful in Christ Jesus' (which would be the rendering of the Greek if 'at Ephesus' were omitted and nothing put in its place).

V. 2 **Grace to you and peace from God our Father and the Lord Jesus Christ.**—The regular Greek greeting was 'Rejoice!' (*chaire*); the regular Jewish greeting was 'Peace!'[2] Paul commonly combines the two, but he likes to replace *chaire* by the similarly-sounding but richer greeting *charis* ('grace'). The regular collocation of 'the Lord Jesus Christ' with 'God our Father' as the source of these blessings bears eloquent witness to the place which Paul and other early Christians gave to our Lord in confession and worship.

2. A DOXOLOGY (1. 3-14)

The doxology with which this new paragraph begins is amplified by Paul's contemplation of God's eternal purpose (verses 4-12), and this leads him on in turn to contemplate the wonder of the unity of Jew and Gentile in Christ (verses 13-14).

V. 3 **Blessed** *be* **the God and Father of our Lord Jesus Christ, who hath blessed us with every spiritual blessing in the heavenly** *places* **in Christ:**—A similar ascription of

---

[1] One of the Chester Beatty Biblical papyri. Papyrus 46, containing most of the Pauline epistles and Hebrews, is dated about A.D. 200.

[2] In Hebrew, *shalom* (cf. Arabic *salaam*); in Greek, *eirēnē*.

blessing follows the salutation in 2 Cor. 1. 3 and 1 Pet. 1. 3; the explicit reason for praising 'the God and Father of our Lord Jesus Christ' varies in accordance with the purpose and theme of the epistle. Here the keynote of the Epistle to the Ephesians is struck at once. The writer and his readers are 'in Christ'—members of Christ, sharers of His resurrection-life—and because Christ Himself is now exalted in the heavenly realm, those who are 'in Him' belong to that heavenly realm, too, in the mind of God. It is there that they enjoy 'every spiritual blessing' that God has bestowed upon them as the people of Christ. Temporally they continue to live here on earth; spiritually they live already in the heavenly realm where Christ lives. It is this twofold relation that constitutes the special tension of Christian existence in the world between the two advents.

The 'heavenly places' in which believers receive the divine blessings 'in Christ' are mentioned in four other places in this epistle. From these the character of these regions in or above the heavens (Gk. *ta epourania*) may be more fully gathered. They constitute the sphere to which the risen Christ has been exalted, where He sits enthroned at God's right hand (1. 20), where those who have died and risen with Christ sit along with Him (2. 6), where principalities and powers see the many-hued wisdom of God exhibited through the church (3. 10), and where spiritual forces of wickedness must be resisted and vanquished by believers armed with the panoply of God (6. 12). The adjective *epouranios* occurs several times in the New Testament, but this particular use of the neuter plural is specially characteristic of Ephesians.

Spiritual blessings are those which are appropriate to people who have their true home in the heavenly realm; they are the Christian counterpart to those temporal blessings which the Old Testament promised to those who were pressing on to an earthly inheritance (cf. Deut. 28. 1-14).

2a. *The Mystery of God's Eternal Purpose* (1. 4-12)

V. 4 even as he chose us in him before the foundation of the world,—So far as the personal experience of believers is

concerned, their entry into the relationship described by the words
'in Christ' took place when they were born from above, and was
symbolized in baptism; but from God's point of view it has no
such temporal limitation. They have been objects of His eternal
choice, and that eternal choice is so completely bound up with
the person of Christ that in the light of the divine purpose they
are described as being 'in Christ' before the world's foundation.[1]
Here we are confronted by the mystery of God's grace. In the
presence of such mystery we do well to be humble, acknowledging
the limitations of our own understanding and paying heed to the
solemnly practical purpose of God's electing grace—

**that we should be holy and without blemish before him
in love:**—The punctuation of the marginal variant in R.V. ('that
we should be holy and without blemish before him: having in
love foreordained us . . .') is probably to be preferred to the
punctuation given in the text. In any case, the purpose which
God had in view in making choice of His people in Christ was
nothing short of their entire sanctification. True, this purpose
will not be fully realized until the resurrection: 'we know that, if
he shall be manifested, we shall be like him; for we shall see him
as he is' (1 John 3. 2). But the glorification which awaits believers on that day is the completion of that sanctification which is
wrought within them by the Spirit now; it is the will of God
that those who are 'in Christ' should also be like Christ—in increasing measure here, in fulness hereafter. The predestinating love
of God is commended more by those who lead holy and Christ-like
lives than by those whose attempts to unravel the mystery partake
of the nature of logic-chopping.

V. 5 **having foreordained us unto adoption as sons
through Jesus Christ unto himself,**—The words 'in love' at
the end of verse 4 should probably come at the beginning of this

---

[1] An attempt is sometimes made to interpret the phrase *katabolē kosmou*, here
translated 'the foundation of the world', as 'the downfall of the world', and to
link it up with the catastrophic interpretation of Gen. 1. 2. Whatever be the
interpretation of Gen. 1. 2, it is certain that *katabolē* can mean nothing but
'laying down' in the sense of 'establishing' or 'founding'; the phrase used here
and in ten other New Testament passages is unambiguous and denotes the
creation of the universe.

verse, closely attached to the verb 'having foreordained'. This foreordination is part of what is involved in our pre-mundane election in Christ. God marked us out in advance as those who were to receive a highly honoured status as His sons.[1] This 'adoption' is more than our relationship to God as His children which is ours by the new birth; it embraces all the privileges and responsibilities which belong to those whom God has acknowledged as His freeborn, full-grown sons. It is a status which we receive in Christ our Redeemer, through faith (Gal. 3. 26; 4. 5); which we appropriate in practice through obedience to the Spirit's guidance (Rom. 8. 14 f.; Gal. 4. 6 f.); which will be given full and universal recognition at the Second Advent of Christ, for the day when the *Son* of God is revealed will also be the day of 'the revealing of the *sons* of God' (Rom. 8. 19). And when that day dawns, Paul assures us, all creation will share in its joy. God's foreordaining some to be His sons does not shut His other creatures out from blessing, but is the very means of their ultimate blessing, and that on a cosmic scale (Rom. 8. 21). What a poverty-stricken view of God's predestinating grace is taken by those who think of it solely in terms of being sealed for heaven and delivered from hell! It is, moreover, 'through Jesus Christ'—through the eternal Son of God—that we have been predetermined as sons of God; and God's ultimate object in so predetermining us is His own glory: He has foreordained us 'unto Himself'.

according to the good pleasure of his will,—The ground of God's choice, of His foreordaining us to be His sons, cannot be found in us. It was not because He foresaw something accept-

---

[1] The word 'adoption' (Gk. *hyiothesia*) is used by Paul alone of the New Testament writers, and by him five times; the other occurrences are Rom. 8. 15, 23; 9. 4; Gal. 4. 5. An important study of 'Adoption in the Pauline Corpus', contributed to *The Evangelical Quarterly* 28 (1956), pp. 6 ff., by Professor D. J. Theron, concludes that the roots of Paul's use of the term are to be found 'in the Jewish rather than in the Graeco-Roman or other traditions. It might even have been derived from Israel's deliverance out of bondage in Egypt. Adoption seems to be the most comprehensive concept that Paul employed of man's restoration. Adoption involves a crisis in the life of the believer followed by a process and it points to an eschatological completion. The ultimate purpose of adoption is the restoration of man to freedom and to a harmonious relationship with God his Father.'

able in us, not even because He foreknew that we would believe the gospel, that He singled us out for such an honour as this. The ground must be sought exclusively in His own gracious character: being the God He is, He willed and decreed our adoption as His sons, our conformity to His image, and in the fulness of time He sent His Son through whom alone this loving purpose could be made effective.

V. 6 **to the praise of the glory of his grace, which he freely bestowed on us in the Beloved**:—The multiplication of genitival phrases like 'the praise of the glory of his grace' is a noteworthy feature of the style of this Epistle, especially where Paul wishes to emphasize the superlative majesty of God's grace and glory and wisdom and power. The grace of God in redeeming sinful children of Adam and adopting them as His own sons will be throughout eternity the most glorious theme of praise to His name. And with this grace, says the apostle, He has 'be-graced' us in the Beloved—for thus we may literally translate the verb *charitoō*, rendered 'freely bestowed' in R.V. 'The Beloved' (corresponding to 'the Son of His love' in Col. 1. 13) is probably a recognized messianic designation. We may compare the voice which our Lord heard at His baptism: 'Thou art my son, *my beloved*, in Thee I am well pleased' (Mark 1. 11). Variant renderings of what is basically one and the same messianic title appear elsewhere in the New Testament; thus God's Beloved is also His 'chosen One' (cf. Luke 9. 35, R.V.) and 'His own One' (Acts 20. 28).[1] Be it noted again that all the blessings which are ours by God's grace are ours *in Christ*; there is no way apart from Him in which God either decrees or effects the bestowal of His grace on men.

V. 7 **in whom we have our redemption through his blood, the forgiveness of our trespasses, according to the riches of his grace,**—As he contemplates God's grace conveyed to us in Christ, Paul enumerates some of the blessings which we owe to that grace (possibly using the language of a primitive

---

[1] Translating 'the blood of His own One' rather than 'His own blood'.

Christian confession of faith). Among these blessings is our 'redemption' (Gk. *apolytrōsis*)—the redemption which we have *in Christ*, because it is only as those who share His risen life that we have made effective *in* us what He has done *for* us. This redemption is something that He has procured on our behalf; the word implies that our former existence was one of slavery from which we required to be ransomed. The ransom-price is expressly mentioned (as it is not in the best-authenticated texts of the parallel passage in Col. 1. 14); it was a price of immeasurable costliness, nothing less than the blood of Christ (cf. Rom. 3. 24 f.; 1 Pet. 1. 18 f.). If, even under the shadow-economy of the Levitical ritual, sacrificial blood was accepted for the worshippers' atonement 'by reason of the life' (Lev. 17. 11), then the price at which our emancipation was purchased was the infinitely more acceptable life of the Incarnate Son, freely offered up on the cross as a sacrifice to God in behalf of men. With this redemption our forgiveness is closely linked, as in the words of Jesus in Matt. 26. 28: 'this is my blood of the covenant, which is shed for many unto remission of sins'. Here it is our 'trespasses' (Gk. *paraptōma*, 'falling by the way', 'false step', 'deviation') that are remitted; in Col. 1. 14 (as in Matt. 26. 28, just quoted) the word is 'sins' (Gk. *hamartia*, 'missing the mark', the most general term in the New Testament for failure to conform to God's will). Both terms denote the same ugly reality under slightly differing figures; in either case pardon and restoration are freely granted to us in Christ, so rich is His grace.

V. 8 **which he made to abound toward us in all wisdom and prudence,**—That the 'manifold wisdom of God' is displayed to the universe by means of His redeemed people is something which Paul affirms later in this letter (Eph. 3. 10). But here it is more likely that the 'wisdom and prudence' are gifts which the believer receives in consequence of the divine grace. Not only are redemption and forgiveness bestowed on us, but spiritual wisdom (Gk. *sophia*) and discernment (Gk. *phronēsis*) are imparted as well, so that we may grasp something of the divine purpose of the ages and of the place which we occupy therein. In 1 Cor. 2. 6 Paul says that he speaks wisdom among those who are full-grown, but he could not teach it to the Corinthians because of their spiritual immaturity. Here, however, he brings to light that 'hidden wisdom which God foreordained before the world unto our glory' (1 Cor. 2. 7).

V.9 **having made known unto us the mystery of his will, according to his good pleasure which he purposed in him** —In this Epistle as elsewhere in the New Testament, a 'mystery' is something hitherto concealed but now unveiled.[1] Here Paul speaks of a purpose which God has set before Himself—a purpose conceived in Christ and to be fulfilled in Christ—of which at best only faint adumbrations had hitherto been perceived. But now it has been revealed in its glorious fulness, first to Paul, and then through Paul to the Church at large. What this fulness comprises we may learn in greater detail as we continue to read this Epistle; in the present place Paul sums it up concisely.

V. 10 **unto a dispensation of the fulness of the times, to sum up all things in Christ, the things in the heavens, and the things upon the earth**;—There is no punctuation between this verse and the preceding one (see R.V.). The progress of Paul's thought may be expressed by such a paraphrase as the following, beginning in the middle of verse 9: 'And this is in accordance with God's purpose which has its origin and its accomplishment in the person of Christ—a purpose to be carried into effect when the time is ripe for it—that all things, in heaven and on earth alike, should find their one true head in Christ'. This is the grand purpose of God which embraces all lesser aspects of His purpose within itself—the establishment of a new order, a new creation, of which Christ shall be the acknowledged head. If here and now Christ is 'head over all things to the church' (verse 22), this is a promise of the day when He

---

[1] The 'wonderful mysteries' of God are frequently mentioned in the Qumran literature, and there too they have reference to the purpose of God, to be fulfilled in the end-time. But with Paul this fulfilment is bound up with Christ; indeed, Christ *is* 'the mystery of God' (Col. 2. 2). An exhaustive comparison of the Qumran literature with Paul's epistles (and not least with Colossians and Ephesians) has still to be made. See p. 65, n. 1; p. 106, n. 1.

will be head of a completely redeemed creation. We have a parallel thought in Jas. 1. 18: 'Of his own will he brought us forth by the word of truth, that we should be a kind of firstfruits of his creatures'. The word translated 'dispensation' is *oikonomia*, which properly means 'stewardship' or 'administration'; it is used here of the administration of God's grand purpose, the putting of that purpose into effect. The 'fulness of the times' (cf. 'the fulness of the time' in Gal. 4. 4) denotes the completion of an appointed period of time and hence the arrival of a new epoch. At the end of one appointed period of time God sent forth His Son (Gal. 4. 4); when all the times and seasons which the Father has fixed by His own authority have run their course, God's age-long purpose which He planned in Christ will attain its full fruition. Everything in heaven and earth will then be summed up in Christ; the verb used is *anakephalaioō* (to 'head up', 'sum up' or 'recapitulate'), which here implies 'the entire harmony of the universe, which shall no longer contain alien and discordant elements, but of which all the parts shall find their centre and bond of union in Christ'.[1]

in him, *I say,*—These final words of verse 10 are to be taken closely together with the opening words of verse 11.

V. 11 **in whom also we were made a heritage,**—This is a preferable rendering to that of A.V., 'in whom also we have obtained an inheritance'. Both statements are true, but the apostle is thinking here of 'God's own possession' (verse 14), 'his inheritance in the saints' (verse 18). So, in Old Testament days, it was revealed that 'the LORD's portion is his people; Jacob is the lot of his inheritance' (Deut. 32. 9). In Christ, then, we have been admitted to the ranks of the chosen people, the holy heritage of God.

having been foreordained according to the purpose of him who worketh all things after the counsel of his will;—As in verse 5 believers are said to have been foreordained 'unto adoption as sons', so here it is implied that their inclusion in the heritage of God was an object of divine foreordination. From all

---

[1] J. B. Lightfoot, *Notes on the Epistles of St. Paul* (1895), p. 322.

3

eternity it was the purpose of God to bring into being a community of men and women who would be in a peculiar sense His own possession. And whatever God has purposed is sure of fulfilment; He is described here as the One 'who worketh all things after the counsel of his will'. That is to say, when once His will has decreed that something shall be so, His wisdom and power and love combine to order and overrule the course of events so that all things are made to work together for the accomplishment of what He has planned. Even sin and other evils, however contrary to His will, can be turned by Him to serve His purposes of glory and blessing. This is pre-eminently manifested by the way in which that sin of sins, the rejection and murder of His incarnate Son, has become in His hands the means by which all the blessings of the gospel are secured to those who believe.

V. 12 **to the end that we should be unto the praise of his glory, we who had before hoped in Christ**:—However we may contemplate the foreordaining purpose of God, His own glory is displayed therein—in its conception as well as in its accomplishment. In verse 6 the foreordination of believers to adoption as sons tends 'to the praise of the glory of his grace'; so here their foreordination to be His special heritage means that 'the praise of his glory' will shine forth in them: that is to say, the glory of God unveiled in His people is to draw forth the admiring praise of the universe (cf. Eph. 3. 10). It is plain that in verses 11 and 12 Paul has primarily in mind believers of Jewish origin, the more immediate heirs of 'the covenants of the promise'. It has, indeed, been suggested that the term 'before' in the clause 'who had before hoped in Christ' means 'before the summing up' of verse 10, in which case the expression would embrace all who are to believe in Christ before the grand consummation. But the words 'ye also' in verse 13, with their evident allusion to Gentile Christians, indicate clearly enough that 'we' in verses 11 and 12 are Jewish Christians. They represent the people of God, the believing remnant of Israel, whose hope was fixed on the Messiah before He came, and who accepted Him when He appeared either immediately (like the original disciples) or after an interval (like

Paul himself). The gospel order, 'to the Jew first, and also to
the Greek' (Rom. 1. 16; cf. 2. 9 f.), is illustrated historically by
the fact that for the first few years after the death and resurrection
of Christ, the message of life through faith in Him was proclaimed
'to none save only to Jews' (Acts 11. 19); its direct presentation
to Gentiles marks a second stage in its progress.

2b. *The Unity of Jew and Gentile in Christ* (1. 13-14)

V. 13 **in whom ye also, having heard the word of the
truth, the gospel of your salvation,**—After 'ye also' we should
supply 'were made a heritage' (understood from verse 11). Paul
points the distinction between Jewish believers ('we') and Gentile
believers ('ye also') in order to bring out more fully the central
emphasis of this epistle—that Gentile believers have been incorporated along with Jewish believers as members of the body
of Christ and sharers of the heritage of God. In the old order
there were blessings enjoyed by Israel in which the Gentiles
had no part; in the new order there is no blessing enjoyed by a
Jewish believer to which a Gentile believer has not an equal
claim. Perhaps today, when Gentile Christianity has been pre-
dominant for so many centuries, it may be necessary to reverse
that statement and insist that in the new order there is no blessing
enjoyed by a Gentile believer to which a Jewish believer has not
an equal claim. One way or the other, there are no second-class
members of the Church of Christ. The message which Paul's
Gentile readers heard is called 'the word of the truth' because it
proceeds from the God of truth and conveys the highest truth
that He has to reveal; it is called 'the gospel of your salvation'
because, as they knew very well from their own experience of it,
it was the good news which brought the way of salvation home to
them.

**—in whom, having also believed, ye were sealed with the
Holy Spirit of promise,**—The phrase 'in whom' does not so
much imply that Christ was the One in whom they believed (that
was true, of course), as that He was the One in whom they were
sealed with the Spirit. The sealing with the Spirit is not an

isolated and individual matter; it has reference to the new life
which they share 'in Christ' with all their fellow-believers. The
words 'having also believed' mean 'when you Gentiles believed
in your turn, as we Jewish Christians had already done'. The
participle 'having believed' is identical with that occurring in
Paul's question to the disciples at Ephesus in Acts 19. 2: 'Did ye
receive the Holy Ghost *when ye believed*?' It is called by grammarians the 'coincident' aorist participle because it denotes an
action coincident in time with that of the main verb.

What is meant by being 'sealed' with the Holy Spirit?[1] The
expression occurs here and in Eph. 4. 30, where the present
passage is echoed. An owner seals his property with his signet
to mark it as his; if at a later time he comes to claim it and his
right to it is questioned, his seal is sufficient evidence and puts an
end to such questioning. So, the fact that believers are endowed
with the Spirit is the token that they belong in a special sense to
God. If the twelve disciples of Acts 19. 1-7 were among those
who heard this epistle read when it reached its destination, they
would have thought immediately of that day when Paul met
them and told them about the Holy Spirit of whom they had
never heard before, the day when they received the Spirit after
being baptized into the name of the Lord Jesus and having
Paul's hands laid upon them. And others among their fellow-
Christians would similarly think of the day when the Spirit came
upon *them*, although to many of them this had happened as soon
as they believed, before they entered the baptismal water as the
outward and visible sign of the inward and spiritual grace which
they had received.[2] One way or the other, they had thus been
incorporated into that living fellowship which was inaugurated
when the Spirit came down to take possession of the new people
of God on the first Christian Pentecost. Other seals, literal or
figurative (like circumcision, the seal of the covenant with Abraham), were affixed externally; the seal of the new covenant is
imprinted in the believing heart.

---

[1] See G. W. H. Lampe, *The Seal of the Spirit* (London, 1951).
[2] Cf. Acts 10. 44-48.

Then why is the Spirit called 'the Holy Spirit of promise' here and in Eph. 4. 30? Partly, no doubt, because He is the promised Holy Spirit, promised from days of old (compare the prophecy of Joel 2. 28 and its fulfilment according to Acts 2. 16 f.). For this reason the gift of the Spirit is called 'the promise of the Father' in Acts 1. 4—that is to say, the gift which the Father has promised. There 'of the Father' is an example of what grammarians call the 'subjective genitive'; the Father is the One who has made the promise. In Gal. 3. 14 we read of 'the promise of the Spirit', where 'of the Spirit' is an example of the 'objective genitive'; the Spirit is the One who has been promised. But the title here, 'the Holy Spirit of promise', reminds us not only that we are living in the age of the fulfilment of God's promises of old; it reminds us also that our possession of the Spirit is itself a promise that God will bring to final consummation that good work which He has already begun in us.

V. 14 **which is an earnest of our inheritance,**—The possessive pronoun 'our' here includes Jewish and Gentile believers together. The truth which is expressed in one way by the figure of 'sealing' is expressed in another way by the use of the word 'earnest'. This Greek word (*arrhabōn*) is derived from a Semitic root represented in the Hebrew Bible by the term rendered 'pledge' three times in Gen. 38. 17-20. There Judah gave his daughter-in-law Tamar certain articles of his personal property as a pledge until he could redeem his promise to present her with 'a kid of the goats'. The word is used in Modern Greek for an engagement ring, a fact which speaks for itself. So our possession of the Spirit here and now is the guarantee divinely given that we shall one day enjoy in its fulness all that inheritance which God has reserved in heaven for those that love Him (cf. 1 Cor. 2. 9; 1 Pet. 1. 4).

unto the redemption of *God's* **own possession, unto the praise of his glory.**—Believers are God's redeemed possession already, but the consummation of His redeeming work remains to be experienced by us. We 'have the first fruits of the Spirit', but the harvest still lies in the future; meanwhile we are 'waiting

for our adoption, to wit, the redemption of our body' (Rom. 8. 23).
The word for 'God's own possession' (Gk. *peripoiēsis*) appears in
much the same sense in 1 Pet. 2. 9; the corresponding verb is
rendered 'purchased' in Acts 20. 28.   Such Old Testament passages as Exod. 19. 5; Deut. 14. 2; Psa. 74. 2, and Mal. 3. 17, form a
background to these New Testament expressions (cf. also Titus 2.
14, where another word of similar meaning, *periousios*, is used).
Not only our inheritance in Christ, but God's inheritance in the
saints, will be finally realized in that coming age, and 'the praise
of His glory' will be complete.

3. A PRAYER FOR WISDOM (1. 15-2. 10)

V. 15 **For this cause I also, having heard of the faith in
the Lord Jesus which is among you, and which** *ye shew*
toward all the saints,—With these words the apostle introduces
a prayer that his readers may be granted wisdom and spiritual
understanding, so that they may grasp truths which the unregenerate or unenlightened intellect is unable to appreciate.
The reading of this verse in R.V. follows those texts which omit
the words 'the love' (Gk. *tēn agapēn*) between 'and' and 'which
ye shew'.   The weight of the evidence favours the omission;
the longer reading (found, e.g., in A.V.) is probably due to an
assimilation of this verse to the parallel passage in Col. 1. 4.   As
the Thessalonians' faith had gone forth in every place, so the
faith of the Ephesians and other recipients of the present epistle
was a manifest example to all their fellow-Christians.   The news
of it filled the apostle with joy and grateful praise.

V. 16 **cease not to give thanks for you, making mention**
of you **in my prayers**;—This is a recurring note at the beginning
of Paul's epistles; we may compare Rom. 1. 8 f.; 1 Cor. 1. 4;
Phil. 1. 3 f.; Col. 1. 3; 1 Thess. 1. 2; 2 Thess. 1. 3; Philem. 4.
What an intercessor he must have been!

V. 17 **that the God of our Lord Jesus Christ, the Father
of glory, may give unto you a spirit of wisdom and revelation in the knowledge of him**;—Here, then, is his prayer to

God on his converts' behalf. God has already been called 'the God and Father of our Lord Jesus Christ' in verse 3 (although even there the Vatican Codex omits the words 'and Father'); here the title is shortened but the reference to God's Fatherhood is supplied by the added title 'the Father of glory'. By this new title Paul wishes to emphasize the unique glory of God's Fatherhood as the archetypal Fatherhood; as he says it Eph. 3. 15, all fatherhood in heaven or on earth is in one way or another derived from His Fatherhood. He prays that God may impart to them a spirit of wisdom and revelation. While the reference is not actually to the personal Spirit of God here, yet such a spirit of wisdom and revelation cannot be possessed apart from Him who is 'the Spirit of wisdom and understanding, the Spirit of counsel and might, the Spirit of knowledge and of the fear of the LORD' (Isa. 11. 2). Knowledge without wisdom can be a menace; wisdom is that insight into the nature of things, that sense of what is fitting, which enables one to co-ordinate and use one's knowledge aright. Men who know many things are all around us; men of spiritual wisdom are so rare that they are worth far more than their weight in gold. But the knowledge of which the apostle speaks is not primarily a knowledge of things or facts; it is the personal knowledge of God. And this knowledge is impossible unless God is pleased to make Himself known. Hence the spirit which the apostle desires for his readers is a spirit of revelation as well as one of wisdom. 'The things of God none knoweth, save the Spirit of God' (1 Cor. 2. 11); 'but unto us God revealed them through the Spirit: for the Spirit searcheth all things, yea, the deep things of God' (1 Cor. 2. 10). If theology, knowledge *about* God, is impossible without divine revelation, how much more so is that acquaintance with God Himself, that *epignōsis*, of which the apostle speaks here!

V. 18 **having the eyes of your heart enlightened,**—The heart in Scripture is the seat of the intelligence and will, and it is this inward vision which needs to be illuminated by the Spirit if we are to know God and appreciate His revealed truth and His eternal purpose. It is unlikely that the word 'enlightened' here has any direct reference to the early Christian use of 'enlightenment' in the sense of baptism.[1]

that ye may know what is the hope of his calling,—Three things are proposed for spiritual men to learn, and they embrace past, present and future in their scope. The first is the hope of the calling of God. The calling of God finds its source in His choice of His people in Christ before the world's foundation (verse 4); it begins to become effective in personal life when those whom He foreordained to be conformed to the image of His Son respond to His persuasive and enabling call as Christ is freely presented to them in the gospel (Rom. 8. 30); it points on to the hope of ultimate consummation when God's purpose is achieved in His people and they are glorified with Christ. To see Him face to face and to be conformed to His image—what more blessed hope could be set before men than this? And it is to the attainment of this hope that believers have been called.

what the riches of the glory of his inheritance in the saints,—Here is the second thing which they are to learn. The hope of God's calling involves a glorious inheritance for His people, but we must not overlook the fact (of which we have already been reminded in verses 11 and 14) that His people constitute an inheritance for God, His own possession, in whom He will display to the universe the untold riches of His glory. We can scarcely realize what it must mean to God to see His purpose complete, to see creatures of His hand, sinners redeemed by His grace, reflecting His own glory.

3a. *God's Power in the Raising of Christ from the Dead*
(1. 19-23)

V. 19 **and what the exceeding greatness of his power to us-ward who believe, according to that working of the strength of his might**—The third thing which the apostle desires his readers to know is the power of God. But when he thinks of the power of God, he presses all the terms for power

---

[1] See note on Eph. 5. 14 (p. 108).

in his vocabulary into service in order to convey something of its all-surpassing character. Paul is the only New Testament writer to use this participle translated 'exceeding' (Gk. *hyper-ballōn*), and he does so in five places altogether. In the other four it is used of the surpassing glory of the new covenant (2 Cor. 3. 10), the grace of God manifested in His people's liberality (2 Cor. 9. 14), the riches of God's grace displayed 'in kindness toward us in Christ Jesus' (Eph. 2. 7), and 'the love of Christ which passeth knowledge' (Eph. 3. 19). But not content with this superlative word, he piles synonym on synonym as he describes how God's 'power' (*dynamis*) operates according to the inworking (*energeia*) of the strength (*kratos*) of His might (*ischys*). Why this attempt to exhaust the resources of language to convey something of the greatness of God's power? Because he is thinking of one supreme occasion when that power was exerted.

V. 20 **which he wrought in Christ, when he raised him from the dead,**—When the New Testament writers wish to show the fulness of God's love, they point to the death of Christ. 'God commendeth his own love toward us, in that, while we were yet sinners, Christ died for us' (Rom. 5. 8). But if the death of Christ is the chief demonstration of the love of God, the chief demonstration of His power is the resurrection of Christ. And it is specially important that believers should know the power of God, because the power by which He raised Jesus from the dead is 'the power that worketh in us' (Eph. 3. 20), the power by which we are enabled to repudiate the dominion of sin and walk with Christ 'in newness of life' (Rom. 6. 4-14). (Compare Paul's prayer in Phil. 3. 10 that he himself might come to know Christ 'and the power of his resurrection'.)

and made him to sit at his right hand in the heavenly *places*,—But the raising of Christ from the dead was but the first stage in His exaltation. God raised Him not only from the sepulchre but raised Him higher still to share His throne. From the earliest days of the apostolic preaching the resurrection and enthronement of Christ were proclaimed side by side as integral to the good news, and both were interpreted as the fulfilment of prophecy. Thus Peter, on the first Christian Pentecost, announced the resurrection of Christ as the fulfilment of Psa. 16. 10 and His enthronement at God's right hand as the fulfilment of Psa. 110. 1, and declared that this twofold fulfilment put it beyond question that the same Jesus whom his hearers had crucified was both Lord and Messiah (Acts 2. 25-36). The demonstration of the power of God was also the vindication of the Lordship of Christ.

V. 21 **far above all rule, and authority, and power, and dominion, and every name that is named,**—When the biblical writers spoke of the right hand of God, they knew as well as we do that God has no material body, and that His right hand is a figurative expression for the place of highest honour and authority. This is what Paul brings out in the words that follow. Christ is enthroned above the universe. As the Queen was reminded at her coronation when the orb was placed in her hand, 'When you see this orb set under the cross, remember that the whole world is subject to the power and empire of Christ our Redeemer'. In the divine administration of the world there are many grades of authority, human and superhuman; Christ is above them all. He is above them all in the order of creation, for they were all created by Him, as Col. 1. 16 emphasizes; He is above them all in order of redemption, for to Him as the suffering and triumphant Son of Man God has given universal sovereignty (Dan. 7. 13 f.). It is not necessary to draw fine distinctions between the terms 'rule, and authority, and power, and dominion'; what is meant is that, whatever forms of government there may be and whatever names they may bear, they must confess the supremacy of Him whom God has highly exalted, and to whom He has given 'the name which is above every name' (Phil. 2. 9 f.).

not only in this world, but also in that which is to come: —Whatever differences in administration may appear between this age and the coming age, they will involve no diminution of the sovereignty of Christ. On the contrary, His sovereignty will be more openly manifested and more universally acknowledged

then than it is now. For the 'world-rulers of this darkness', who
are mentioned in Eph. 6. 12, exercise considerable control over
men and nations in the present age, but in the coming age their
control will be a thing of the past.[1] For Christ must reign till 'he
shall have abolished all rule and all authority and power . . . till
he hath put all his enemies under his feet' (1 Cor. 15. 24 f.).

V. 22 **and he put all things in subjection under his feet,**—
Here, as in Heb. 2. 6 ff., the words of Psa. 8. 6, first applied to
Adam as he left the creative hand of God, are applied to the Second
Man who has broken the deadly entail of the fall and by His
redemptive work won the sovereignty which is His as Head of the
new creation. As is pointed out in 1 Cor. 15. 27 and Heb. 2. 8,
the complete fulfilment of these words in Christ will not come
until death itself is destroyed and God is all in all; but Christ's
present enthronement at God's right hand is assurance enough
that this blessed consummation will come without fail.

and gave him to be head over all things to the church,—
The crown rights of the Redeemer are twofold. He is not only by
divine decree 'the head of all principality and power' (Col. 2. 10)
and 'ruler of the kings of the earth' (Rev. 1. 5); He also bears a
unique relation to the new community that has been called into
being by His death and exaltation. He is, by the appointment of
His Father, 'head over all things to the church'. The expression
'head over all things' is as much as to say 'supreme head'. But
the title 'head' is used here in a much richer sense than that which
it bears in the passage just quoted from Col. 2. 10, where Christ
is described as 'head of all principality and power'. There the
title denotes His sovereign authority; it is from Him (as the One
to whom all authority has been given in heaven and on earth) that
all power in the universe is derived. But here it means all this and
much besides; it expresses a vital unity. For the Church over
which Christ has been appointed supreme head is the Church—

V. 23 **which is his body,**—This is the first occasion on which

---

[1] Compare also Heb. 2. 5: this world is subjected to angelic powers, but not
'the world to come'; it is the domain of the Son of Man. On the whole subject
see G. B. Caird, *Principalities and Powers* (London, 1956).

the word 'church' (Gk. *ekklēsia*) appears in this epistle. In the
Septuagint, the pre-Christian translation of the Old Testament
into Greek, *ekklēsia* is used as an equivalent of Heb. *qāhāl*
('assembly')—the people of Israel viewed as a religious community. We are prepared for a change in the scope of the word
when we hear our Lord saying in Matt. 16. 18: 'upon this rock I
will build my church'—the reference being to the new *ekklēsia*
consisting of those who, like Peter, confessed Him as Messiah
and Lord. When *ekklēsia* is used in a Christian sense in the New
Testament, it most usually denotes the company of believers in
Christ in some particular place—what we call a particular or local
church. But there are a few passages (and this is one of them)
where the term is used without any local restriction—as indeed it
is used by our Lord Himself in Matt. 16. 18.

The Church of the New Testament is both old and new. It is
old because of its living continuity with the people of God of
Old Testament times (cf. Eph. 2. 19); it is new because it has
died and risen with Christ into a new life in which the limitations
of the past are left behind.

The conception of the Church as the body of Christ is peculiar
to the Pauline epistles in the New Testament.[1] What led Paul to
think of the Church in this way is a matter of considerable debate,
but the essential thought which the figure conveys—the living
power which unites the people of Christ to Him and to one
another—was borne in upon the apostle's mind on the Damascus
road when he heard the voice which said: 'why persecutest thou
me?' In some of his earlier epistles (see 1 Cor. 10. 17; 12. 12-27;
Rom. 12. 4 f.), Paul develops the idea in relation to the harmonious
functioning of believers within the Church as fellow-members
of one body—the body of Christ. But in those earlier epistles
Christ is not viewed as the head of this body. On the contrary,
when Paul elaborates the figure of the body in 1 Cor. 12, he com-
pares an individual believer to the head (verse 21) or to part of the

---

[1] On this subject see J. A. T. Robinson, *The Body* (London, 1952), and E.
Best, *One Body in Christ* (London, 1955).

head (verse 16) as much as to any other member of the body. It is in Colossians and Ephesians that we find this further stage in the unfolding of the figure, in which Christ appears as the head from whom the other parts of the body derive life and power. All the aspects of Christ's exaltation to the right hand of God are important, but the particular aspect which is important for Paul's present purpose in His supremacy as 'the head of the body, the church; who is the beginning, the first-born from the dead; that in all things he might have the pre-eminence' (Col. 1. 18). In the companion epistle to Colossae, from which these words are taken, the pre-eminence of Christ in creation and resurrection is emphasized; in the present epistle Paul draws out, more fully than he does there, the implications of Christ's exaltation for those who are members of His body.

the fulness of him that filleth all in all.—The term 'fulness' (*plērōma*) has a wide range of meaning in the New Testament. In the Gospels it is used of the patch which 'fills up' the rent in an old garment (Matt. 9. 16; Mark 2. 21) and of the left-over fragments which filled several baskets after the two miraculous feedings (Mark 6. 43; 8. 20). In 1 Cor. 10. 26 it is used in a quotation from Psa. 24. 1, to denote the 'fulness' of the earth—i.e. everything that is in it. In Colossians it is applied to Christ as the One in whom the fulness of the Godhead is embodied (Col. 2. 9; cf. 1. 19); and some expositors consider that this is the sense here—that Christ is the 'fulness' of God.[1] In that case the words 'which is his body' must be taken as a parenthesis. But that involves a rather awkward construction, and it is more probable that 'fulness', like 'body', refers to 'the church'. In this case the Church is described as the fulness or complement of Christ, jus' as the body is the necessary complement of the head in order t(make up a complete man. The thought is rather similar to tha in Col. 2. 10: 'and in him ye are made full'. According to R.V. Christ is then referred to as the One 'that filleth all in all'. If thi is the proper translation, it anticipates Eph. 4. 9, where Christ i

---

[1] Cf. C. F. D. Moule, *Colossians and Philemon* (Cambridge, 1957), p. 168.

said to have 'ascended far above all the heavens, that he might fill all things'. Here the wording is more emphatic: He 'fills all things in all things'—i.e. He completely fills the universe.

But there is an alternative rendering to the familiar one. Whereas in Eph. 4. 9 the verb 'fill' is in the active voice, here 'filleth' represents a Greek form of the verb which may be construed either as the middle voice or as the passive. If it is the middle voice, then the force is that of doing something in one's own interest, and the leading English versions (A.V., R.V., R.S.V., etc.) understand it thus, as also did the Syriac versions in antiquity. The Latin versions, however, took it as passive, and so do a number of modern exegetes. In that case the closing words of verse 23 would mean 'the fulness of Him who, all in all, is being filled'—but what does this mean? One suggestion is that God has made Christ Head of the body 'which in turn fulfils and completes Him; for to an absolute completeness he is still moving on' (J. A. Robinson). That is to say, the body of Christ (or, as it might be put, 'Christ corporate') is still advancing toward ultimate completeness. But a more probable interpretation of the passive voice would be to take it as denoting the fact that in Christ the fulness of deity is perpetually resident. The grammatical problem will probably never reach a universally agreed solution, and we may content ourselves for the present with the rendering of the English versions. The Church, the body of Christ, is the complement of Him who fills the entire universe. Elsewhere in his epistles, Paul shows how the members of Christ recapitulate His experience of death, burial and resurrection (Rom. 6. 3-11; Col. 2. 11-13); this is one way in which they may be called His complement or fulness. In this epistle Paul enlarges on this idea (with an interesting modification) and carries it farther than he has done before. Not only do the members of Christ share His risen life; they share His exaltation at God's right hand. This is the subject which he develops in the verses that follow.

CHAPTER II

3b. *God's Power in the Raising of Those who were Dead in Sins (2. 1-10)*

V. 1 **And you** *did he quicken*, **when ye were dead through your trespasses and sins,**—Not only did God raise Christ from the dead by His mighty power; He has raised the people of Christ from the dead as well. This theme of rising-with-Christ is not new in Paul's letters. But in the other places where it appears, rising-with-Christ is the sequel to death-with-Christ and burial-with-Christ. Here the apostle departs from this pattern; in the present passage the death from which God has 'quickened us together with Christ' (verse 5) is not our death-with-Christ but our moral and spiritual death brought about through our trespasses and sins.[1] This modification of the usual sequence of his thought has been felt by some to be so strange that they have suggested that the dative case (*tois paraptōmasin kai tais hamartiais hymōn*) should not be taken as instrumental but in the sense 'dead *to* your trespasses and sins' (cf. Rom. 6. 2, 11). But this suggestion is excluded by the grammatical consideration that the present participle in the phrase 'being dead' (Gk. *ontas nekrous*) here and in verse 5 must refer to the condition existing at the time when the quickening took place. R.V. rightly brings out the force of the present participle by its rendering 'when ye were dead'.[2]

V. 2 **wherein aforetime ye walked according to the course of this world,**—Paul here begins a characteristic digression, suggested by his reference to 'trespasses and sins', before he has completed the first clause of his new paragraph. The interrupted clause is not resumed until verse 5 (from which our translation borrows the phrase 'did he quicken', which appears in italics in verse 1, to help out the sense). The ethical sense of the

---

[1] For the terms 'trespasses' and 'sins' cf. Eph. 1. 7 with accompanying exposition (p. 31).
[2] Compare the similar force of the present participle in Rom. 5. 10: 'being enemies, we were reconciled'.

verb 'to walk' is common in the New Testament. 'The course
of this world' is literally 'the age (*aiōn*) of this world order
(*kosmos*)'; it means what Paul calls 'this present evil age (*aiōn*)'
in Gal. 1. 4. Temporally believers on earth still live in this age,
but spiritually they belong to the new age introduced by the work
of Christ, and they manifest its power in their lives.

according to the prince of the power of the air,—The
devil is here described as the ruler whose authority is exercised
in the realm of the air; i.e. he is the leader of those 'spiritual hosts
of wickedness in the heavenly places' of whom we are told in
Eph. 6. 12. (Another, but less likely, suggestion is that 'air' is
here equivalent to 'darkness' in Luke 22. 53; Eph. 6. 12; Col. 1.
13; since the word used is not *aithēr*, the clear upper air, but *aēr*,
the obscure, misty lower air.) Believers are liberated from bondage to him and his minions, by virtue of the victory of Christ
(cf. Col. 2. 15); unbelievers are still held in subjection to him and
forced to live in accordance with his God-opposing will.

of the spirit that now worketh in the sons of disobedience;
—By adding the preposition 'of' before 'the spirit', R.V. implies
that the devil is not himself 'the spirit that now worketh in the
sons of disobedience' (which the A.V. and R.S.V. rendering indicates), but that he is the prince or ruler of that spirit. The 'spirit'
in this sense is not a personal force, but means more or less what
we have in mind when we speak of the 'spirit of the age'. The
'spirit of the age', says R.V., is under the control and direction
of the devil (cf. 1 John 5. 19). It is certain that R.V. does more
justice here to the grammatical construction; 'prince' and 'spirit'
are not in apposition to each other in Greek, for 'prince' is
accusative whereas 'spirit' is genitive.

The expression 'sons of disobedience' exemplifies an idiomatic
Semitic way of referring to men whose lives are characterized by
disobedience.[1]   The converse term, 'children of obedience',
appears in 1 Pet. 1. 14.

V. 3 among whom we also all once lived in the lusts of

---

[1] Cf. Eph. 5. 6 (pp. 104 f.).

our flesh, doing the desires of the flesh and of the mind,
—Paul is writing to Christians of Gentile birth, but when he
reminds them that they once lived in accordance with the standards
accepted by the 'sons of disobedience', he makes haste to say that
this was equally true of Christians of Jewish birth, not excluding
himself. The 'desires of the flesh' may take many different forms,
and Paul elsewhere lists the things in which he formerly took
such patriotic and religious pride as samples of his 'confidence
in the flesh' (Phil. 3. 4-6). For the 'flesh', the unregenerate nature
of man, can manifest itself in respectable forms as well as in the
disreputable pursuits of first-century paganism. For 'the mind'
we might substitute 'our minds' or 'our thoughts', in order to
indicate that the Greek word (*dianoia*) is plural here; these are
minds, of course, which have not yet been renewed so as to
approve the will of God (Rom. 12. 2).

and were by nature children of wrath, even as the rest:
—We who were Jews by birth and upbringing, he says, were as
much under the wrath of God as those who were born and reared
as pagans. These few words sum up the argument of Rom. 1.
18-2. 29, where Gentile and Jew alike are shown to have incurred
the revelation of God's wrath from heaven.

V. 4—**but God, being rich in mercy, for his great love
wherewith he loved us,**—The wrath of God, however, is not
the whole of the picture. It provides the background against
which His mercy and love stand out in all their radiance. The
wealth of His mercy and the greatness of His love are emphasized,
because it is entirely thanks to that mercy and love that believers
are no longer exposed to His holy wrath against sin.

V. 5 **even when we were dead through our trespasses,
quickened us together with Christ**—Paul now resumes the
sentence which was broken off short at the end of verse 1, but this
time he says 'us' instead of 'you' (including Jewish as well as
Gentile Christians). We have already observed (in the notes on
verse 1) that the death from which we have been 'quickened
together' with Christ is not here our death with Him but the
death brought about by our trespasses. The verb 'to quicken

together' (Gk. *synzōopoieō*) is probably a Pauline coinage to express a new revelation; it appears also in Col. 2. 13.

(by grace have ye been saved),—This fundamental truth is inserted parenthetically here as Paul presses on with his account of all that God has made His people share with Christ; it is repeated and expanded in verse 8. The perfect tense (Gk. *este sesōsmenoi*) expresses a present state resulting from a past action.

V. 6 **and raised us up with him, and made us to sit with him in the heavenly** *places*, **in Christ Jesus:**—In Eph. 1. 20 we have been shown how the surpassing power of God was displayed when He raised Christ from the dead and made Him to sit at His right hand in the heavenly places. Here a further truth is unfolded: God has also raised the people of Christ along with Him (*synegeirō*) and made them sit with Him (*synkathizō*)[1] in those heavenly places.[2] This goes farther even than what is revealed in the companion-letter to Colossae. There believers are raised with Christ (Col. 2. 12; 3. 1), and are urged to 'seek the things that are above, where Christ is, seated on the right hand of God', for the new life which they possess 'is hid with Christ in God' (Col. 3. 1, 3). But here believers are viewed as being already seated there with Christ, by the act and in the purpose of God. Temporally, indeed, we live on earth so long as we remain in this body; but 'in Christ Jesus' we are seated with Christ where He is. And God, who sees all His creatures as they really are, sees believers 'in Christ Jesus'. The verbs 'quickened', 'raised', 'made to sit', are all in the aorist tense; they express what God has already done for His children in Christ.

V. 7 **that in the ages to come he might shew the exceeding riches of his grace in kindness toward us in Christ Jesus:** —In another epistle Paul declares that on the day of His advent Christ is 'to be glorified in his saints, and to be marvelled at in all

---

[1] Paul is notoriously fond of compounds with the prefix *syn* ('together with'); cf. Eph. 3. 6 with accompanying exposition and note (p. 62).

[2] Compare the vision in Dan. 7, where 'one like unto a son of man' receives universal and everlasting dominion (verses 13 f.), with the interpretation that follows it, where it is 'the saints of the Most High' who receive the kingdom and possess it for ever (verse 18).

them that believed' (2 Thess. 1. 10). But here his thought goes beyond that: in the limitless future, as age succeeds age, the crowning display of God's grace will ever be His kindness to His redeemed people, not simply in pardoning their sins, but in raising them up to share the place which Christ occupies by right in the heavenly sphere. The superlative term *hyperballōn*, used here to describe the riches of God's grace, was commented on in our note on Eph. 1. 19, where it describes the greatness of His power. If the raising of Christ from death to sit at His own right hand is the supreme demonstration of God's power, the raising of the people of Christ from spiritual death to share Christ's place of exaltation is the supreme demonstration of His grace.

V. 8 **for by grace have ye been saved through faith**; **and that not of yourselves**: *it is* **the gift of God**:—The parenthesis of verse 5 is now repeated at greater length. In verse 5 'grace' lacks the article in Greek; here it is supplied, for it points back to the grace already mentioned in verses 5 and 7. This is one of the great evangelical summaries of the New Testament. Our salvation springs solely from God's grace and is appropriated by us through faith alone. Not that our faith *merits* the salvation in any way; it is simply the faculty by which we accept the salvation that God's free grace has procured for us. Here is the basis for the watchword of Reformation theology: *sola gratia, sola fide, soli Deo gloria* ('by grace alone, through faith alone, to God alone be glory'). Commentators are not agreed about the exact reference of the words 'and that not of yourselves: it is the gift of God'. Do they refer expressly to faith, or more generally to salvation? It is true, in either case, that we could never exercise saving faith did not the Holy Spirit 'persuade and enable us to embrace Jesus Christ, freely offered to us in the gospel' (to quote the *Westminster Shorter Catechism*). But the fact that the demonstrative pronoun 'that' is neuter in Greek (*touto*), whereas 'faith' is a feminine noun (*pistis*), combines with other considerations to suggest that it is the whole concept of salvation by grace through faith that is described as the gift of God. This, incidentally, was Calvin's interpretation, although many of his followers have preferred to take faith itself as the gift of God here.

V. 9 **not of works, that no man should glory.**—Salvation is not of works, firstly because it is bestowed by grace, and secondly because it is received by faith. 'If it is by grace, it is no more of works: otherwise grace is no more grace' (Rom. 11. 6). 'But to him that worketh not, but believeth on him that justifieth the ungodly, his faith is reckoned for righteousness' (Rom. 4. 5). These and many other Pauline statements of gospel truth are summed up concisely in this passage. If salvation were of works, men would have something to boast about (cf. Rom. 4. 2). But when it is all of grace, and received by faith, all boasting is 'excluded' (Rom. 3. 27); if the Christian wishes to glory, 'let him glory in the Lord' (1 Cor. 1. 31).

V. 10 **For we are his workmanship, created in Christ Jesus for good works, which God afore prepared that we should walk in them.**—But if we are not saved *by* good works, we are assuredly saved *for* good works. For this purpose (among others which this epistle mentions) God fashioned us as His new creation 'in Christ Jesus'. We are His 'workmanship' (Gk. *poiēma*), His work of art, His masterpiece. And we shall show that we are His workmanship by the works which we perform. Those who continue to 'walk' in the trespasses and sins which characterize the unregenerate state show that they are not God's workmanship, whatever professions they may make. But those who 'walk' in those good works which God has preordained for His people give ample evidence of the power of a new life which operates within them. No one more wholeheartedly than Paul repudiated good works as a *ground* of salvation; no one more wholeheartedly insisted on good works as the *fruit* of salvation. The later chapters of this epistle specify in considerable detail the kind of good works which attest God's workmanship.

4. THE GENTILES MADE HEIRS OF THE PROMISES
(2. 11-22)

V. 11 **Wherefore remember,**—It is salutary from time to

time to be reminded of what we were apart from God's grace, in order that we may the better appreciate the riches of His grace and be armed against the temptation of having high thoughts of ourselves.

that aforetime ye, the Gentiles in the flesh, who are called Uncircumcision by that which is called Circumcision, in the flesh, made by hands;—Although circumcision and uncircumcision are alike irrelevant in the new order (cf. Gal. 5. 6; 6. 15), it must be acknowledged that in earlier days circumcision was the external sign of participation in the covenant made with Abraham (Gen. 17. 10-14), and those who lacked it had no claim to the blessings pronounced in that covenant. But in Christ this external sign, formerly so important, can be dismissed as a merely physical, hand-made circumcision, in favour of the 'circumcision not made with hands' (Col. 2. 11), that seal of the Spirit, which Jews and Gentiles alike may receive by faith.

V. 12 **that ye were at that time separate from Christ,**—not only because they had not come to know Him, but also because they had no part or lot in the Messianic people, 'of whom is Christ as concerning the flesh' (Rom. 9. 5).

alienated from the commonwealth of Israel,—'alienated' in the sense of 'aliens'; they had never been anything else. The community of God's people was in those days confined within the national frontiers of Israel, and was restricted to descendants of Jacob, apart from those Gentiles who were admitted as proselytes.

and strangers from the covenants of the promise,—that is, from the covenants bound up with God's promise to Abraham (see Gen. 12. 2 f.; 13. 14 ff.; 15. 1 ff.; 17. 1 ff.; 22. 15 ff.), which He reaffirmed to Isaac (Gen. 26. 2 ff.) and to Jacob (Gen. 28. 13 f.; 35. 9 ff.).

having no hope and without God in the world.—This description of the Gentiles' status before they were reached by God's gracious purpose in Christ is, in a more general sense, a vivid and apt summary of the moral condition of the pagan rank and file in the first-century Graeco-Roman world.

V. 13 **But now in Christ Jesus ye that once were far off**

are made nigh in the blood of Christ.—But 'in Christ Jesus'—as joint-members of the body of Christ—the seemingly impossible has happened; those who were far off from God have been brought near to Him. And the agency by which this has come about is 'the blood of Christ'—His life willingly yielded up in death as a sin-offering on behalf of 'the many' (Isa. 53. 11, 12), embracing Gentiles as well as Jews. In the words 'far off' and 'nigh' we may detect an echo of Isa. 57. 19, quoted more clearly below in verse 17.

V. 14 **For he is our peace, who made both one,**—No iron curtain, colour bar, class distinction or national frontier of today is more absolute than the cleavage between Jew and Gentile was in antiquity. The greatest triumph of the gospel in the apostolic age was that it overcame this long-standing estrangement and enabled Jew and Gentile to become truly one in Christ. Those who enter into peace with God must have peace with one another. And nothing but the gospel can remove the barriers which divide mankind into hostile groups in our own age.

and brake down the middle wall of partition,—It has frequently been suggested that Paul had a literal wall in mind as a tangible symbol of the division between Jews and Gentiles—the wall in the temple area at Jerusalem which separated the court of the Gentiles from the inner courts (into which only Jewish worshippers might enter) and to which notices were affixed in Greek and Latin, warning Gentiles to keep out on pain of death. Paul himself had narrowly escaped death two or three years earlier when a rumour got about that he had violated the sanctity of the holy place by taking a Gentile into one of the inner courts (Acts 21. 28 f.).

V. 15 **having abolished in his flesh the enmity,**—It was as true man, by giving His body in sacrifice on the cross, that Christ annulled the state of war between these two divisions of mankind.

even **the law of commandments** *contained* **in ordinances**;—The elaborate system of legal observances publicly marked the Jew off from the Gentile. In Col. 2. 14 Paul deals with a prior aspect of our Lord's removal of 'the bond written in ordinances that was against us, which was contrary to us'. There the bond which He has cancelled by 'nailing it to His cross' is our signed acknowledgment of indebtedness in respect of the broken law, which hostile forces used to blackmail us into doing their will. Here a further aspect of that cancellation is seen in the disappearance of that which constituted the chief cause of offence between Jew and Gentile. Out of Christ, of course, the cause of offence still persists; in Christ it has ceased to exist.

that he might create in himself of the twain one new man, *so* **making peace**;—The new man here, like the 'full-grown man' of Eph. 4. 13,[1] is the Christian community viewed corporately, the 'new creation' of Gal. 6. 15, in which Jew and Gentile are reconciled in the unity of the body of Christ. He who 'made peace through the blood of his cross' (Col. 1. 20) between God and His people has also made peace among His people, whatever cleavages kept them apart previously.

V. 16 **and might reconcile them both in one body unto God through the cross,**—Again, our Lord's reconciling work, which is presented in its widest scope in Col. 1. 19 ff., is viewed here in particular connection with the relationship between Jew and Gentile. The 'one body' is the body of Christ of which Jewish and Gentile believers are alike members, rather than His 'flesh' (i.e. His physical body) as in verse 15.

having slain the enmity thereby:—i.e. by means of the cross. Compare the first clause of verse 15.

V. 17 **and he came and preached peace to you that were far off, and peace to them that were nigh:**—This verse echoes Isa. 52. 7 ('How beautiful . . . are the feet of him that bringeth good tidings, that publisheth peace')[2] and still more Isa. 57. 19 ('Peace, peace to him that is far off and to him that is near'). Cf. verse 13 and Acts 2. 39. Clearly it is the Gentiles who were 'far off' and the Jews who were 'nigh'; to both alike Christ's own peace has been proclaimed in the Gospel.

V. 18 **for through him we both have our access in one**

---

[1] Compare also the 'new man' of Eph. 4. 24, where, however, the reference is to the Christ-life in the individual believer. In both places 'new' represents Gk. *kainos* (see exposition on pp. 94 f.).

[2] Cf. Eph. 6. 15 (p. 130).

Spirit unto the Father.—This peace does not merely remove hostility; it positively brings Jewish and Gentile believers on one common footing into the presence of God the Father. Under the law the Jew had access to God, but his access was hedged about by strict limitations; the Gentile could have access only by becoming a proselyte. (This is implied even in such passages as 1 Kings 8. 41-43 and Isa. 56. 6 f.) But now through Christ both have free and unrestricted access to God 'in one Spirit'—the Spirit by whom the 'one body' of Eph. 4. 4 is indwelt and empowered. The implications of this verse for the biblical doctrine of the Trinity will not be lost upon the careful reader.[1]

V. 19 **So then ye are no more strangers and sojourners,** —lit. 'foreigners and "strangers within the gates" ' (Gk. *xenoi kai paroikoi*), whose residence among the people of Israel was based on sufferance and not on right.

but ye are fellow-citizens with the saints,—Paul uses three figures to express the unity of Jewish and Gentile believers in the new fellowship which Christ has created: (i) a city; (ii) a family; (iii) a building. As regards the first, he assures his Gentile readers that they have now received a share in the civic privileges of the people of God,[2] by divinely bestowed right. In the Old Testament the designation 'saints' is reserved for members of one nation only. But now the branches have run over the wall, or rather, the wall itself has disappeared, national restrictions have been abolished, and Gentiles as well as Jews are included in God's holy people. All believers, no matter what their natural ancestry may be, inherit the blessings promised to believing Abraham (Gal. 3. 9) and are burgesses of that well-founded city to which he looked forward (Heb. 11. 10, 16).

and of the household of God,—Secondly, instead of being outsiders as they were in their pagan days, they are now God's housemates, full members of His family, on the same basis as the natural children of Abraham who have entered into God's family

---

[1] Cf. Eph. 4. 4-6 with accompanying exposition (pp. 76-81).
[2] For the compound 'fellow-citizens' (Gk. *sympolitai*) see similar compounds in Eph. 2. 5 f.; 3. 6, with accompanying exposition and notes (pp. 49 f., 62).

by 'like precious faith'. On the composition of the household (or house) of God see Heb. 3. 6.

V. 20 **being built upon the foundation of the apostles and prophets,**—Here comes the transition to the third figure, the building (more particularly the temple). Does 'the foundation of the apostles and prophets' mean the foundation laid by the apostles and prophets, or are the apostles and prophets the foundation? Elsewhere Paul says that 'other foundation can no man lay than that which is laid, which is Jesus Christ' (1 Cor. 3. 11). But here the relation of Christ to the building is expressed by another figure (the chief corner stone), and the reference is probably to the apostles and prophets of the first Christian generation as the ascended Lord's foundation-gifts to the church (cf. Eph. 3. 5; 4. 11; 1 Cor. 12. 28). Steadfast adherence to the apostles' teaching, and not the production of an impressive pedigree, is the best evidence of being built on the foundation of the apostles and prophets.

Christ Jesus himself being the chief corner stone;—The Greek term *akrogōniaios* used here is derived from the Septuagint of Isa. 28. 16, a passage quoted in 1 Pet. 2. 6 as a prophecy of Christ and linked in the following verses with two other 'stone' oracles, Psa. 118. 22 and Isa. 8. 14. The corner-stone is cut out beforehand, and not only bonds the structure together when at last it is dropped into place, but serves as a 'stone of testing' to show whether the building has been carried out to the architect's specifications.

V. 21 **in whom each several building, fitly framed together, groweth into a holy temple in the Lord**;—The rendering in R.V., which has just been quoted, suggests that the completed temple will consist of the aggregate of a large number of smaller buildings, rather like the Great Palace of the Byzantine Emperors at Constantinople. This, however, is hardly compatible with the context of the epistle as a whole. Nor does the New Testament appear to envisage the Church Universal as made up of the sum total of particular churches; it appears rather to view each particular church as something complete in itself, the

Church Universal in its local manifestation. The Greek witnesses to the text are fairly evenly divided between *pasa hē oikodomē* (A.V., 'all the building') and the reading without the definite article, *pasa oikodomē* (rendered literally in R.V. margin, 'every building'). But there is some authority elsewhere in the New Testament for the meaning 'all' in a construction of this kind even when the definite article is absent. In any case, what is said to be growing is not so much the material edifice but the work of building which is in process. And the fact that Paul uses the biological verb 'groweth' when speaking of the Church as a building suggests that the conception of the Church as a living organism, the body of Christ, is uppermost in his mind, whatever other figure he may be employing at the moment. The verb translated 'fitly framed together' (Gk. *synarmologeō*) occurs in one other place in the New Testament—in Eph. 4. 16, where it is used of the living union of the various parts of the body. Here the whole building operation has the perfecting of a holy shrine for God as its goal. The idea that Paul has the Ephesian temple of Artemis at the back of his mind as he writes this is highly improbable; the background of his thought and language is much more Biblical.

V. 22 **in whom ye also are builded together for a habitation of God in the Spirit.**—It is in Christ that individual believers find their place in this structure which is rising as the spiritual tabernacle of God. The thought is very similar to that in 1 Pet. 2. 4 f., where believers, by coming to Christ, the living corner-stone, and taking their proper places in relation to Him, 'are built up a spiritual house'. But Paul had expressed the same idea more concisely in an earlier epistle (1 Cor. 3. 16): 'Know ye not that ye are a temple of God, and that the Spirit of God dwelleth in you?' It is not in any tangible structure, but in the midst of His people, that God makes His dwelling-place on earth; it is there that He records His name and promises His blessing (cf. Exod. 20. 24). And in the words 'ye also' Paul repeats his insistence that Gentile believers have a full share in this high privilege.

CHAPTER III

5. THE PRAYER FOR WISDOM RESUMED

(3. 1-13)

V. 1 For this cause I Paul, the prisoner of Christ Jesus in behalf of you Gentiles,—The prayer that his readers might be filled with divine wisdom, which Paul began in Eph. 1. 15 and amplified by a meditation on the greatness of God's power, as displayed both by the raising of Christ from the dead (1. 20-22) and by the quickening of the Gentiles who were dead in sins (2. 1-10), gave way to the digression of 2. 11-22, where the grace of God in making Gentiles fellow-heirs of the covenant-promises is magnified. That prayer is now resumed, but Paul has not completed one sentence before he embarks upon a fresh digression —an account of the mystery of Christ which has been committed to his stewardship (3. 2-13). The words 'for this cause' refer back to the preceding description of God's grace to the Gentiles; since God has so richly blessed them, Paul will pray more earnestly that they may worthily appreciate His grace in Christ. When he speaks of himself as 'the prisoner of Christ Jesus in behalf of you Gentiles', he thinks of his imprisonment as having been incurred in Christ's service, and more particularly of its having been incurred as a direct consequence of his activity as the apostle to the Gentiles. For it was his faithfulness to the special stewardship entrusted to him by Christ that called forth the peculiarly bitter hostility of his Jewish opponents, as a result of which he was attacked in Jerusalem and put on trial before the Roman courts.

5a. *The Mystery of Christ* (3. 2-7)

V. 2—if so be that ye have heard of the dispensation of that grace of God which was given me to you-ward;—The expression 'if so be that' (Gk. *eige*) does not necessarily imply that they might not have heard; it is quite probably a rhetorical way of reminding them of what they knew already.

The dispensation, or rather stewardship (Gk. *oikonomia*), was a special blessing of God's grace which Paul had been appointed to administer—not only the bestowal of salvation on Gentiles as they believed the gospel which Paul proclaimed to them, but their incorporation as full members of the people of God; and this particular aspect of his stewardship Paul discharged by the planting of churches in which Gentile and Jewish converts enjoyed equal privileges *in Christ*, and on no other basis. Again, 'to you-ward' marks out his Gentile readers as recipients of this 'grace'.

V. 3 **how that by revelation was made known unto me the mystery,**—As we saw in our note on Eph. 1. 9, a mystery in the New Testament sense of the word is something hitherto concealed which has now been disclosed. There the mystery of God's will was referred to in the most comprehensive and far-reaching terms; it was stated to be the establishment of a new creation under the headship of Christ. Here a special phase of this mystery is more particularly in Paul's mind, but this phase is itself a mystery—something previously undreamed of but now revealed to Paul and given to him to unfold and also to carry into effect as the divinely-chosen instrument for that purpose. What this special mystery was is stated expressly in verse 6.

as I wrote afore in few words,—Just which passage in his correspondence Paul is here referring to is a matter of some dispute. Most probably, however, he is referring back to what has already been said in the present epistle, especially in such passages as 1. 9 ff. and 2. 19 ff.

V. 4 **whereby, when ye read, ye can perceive my understanding in the mystery of Christ**;—The expression 'the mystery of Christ' occurs also in Col. 4. 3, where Paul describes himself as a prisoner on its account. But the aspect of the mystery of Christ which is prominent in Colossians is the fact that the indwelling Christ is, for Gentile as well as for Jewish believers, the hope of glory; the aspect on which the apostle dwells here is the fact that in Christ Gentiles are fellow-heirs with Jewish believers.

V. 5 **which in other generations was not made known
unto the sons of men, as it hath now been revealed unto his
holy apostles and prophets in the Spirit**;—Of the aspect of
the mystery which is dealt with in the companion-epistle, Paul
says that it 'hath been hid from all ages and generations: but now
hath it been manifested to his saints, to whom God was pleased
to make known what is the riches of the glory of this mystery
among the Gentiles, which is Christ in you, the hope of glory'
(Col. 1. 26 f.). Here he makes a somewhat fuller statement, to
much the same effect, concerning the concealment hitherto of
that aspect of the divine mystery which he is dealing with now.
Let us consider carefully, however, what it was that was not
made known formerly. That God's blessing was to extend to
the Gentiles as well as to the Jews was a recurrent theme of Old
Testament prophecy, from the promise to Abraham in Gen. 12. 3
onwards. In Rom. 15. 9-12 Paul quotes a string of passages
from all three divisions of the Old Testament (the Law, the
Prophets and the Writings) in which he finds foreshadowings of
the result of his own apostolic ministry among the Gentiles. We
may compare his quotation of Isa. 49. 6 in Acts 13. 47. But what
was not foreseen in Old Testament times was the fact that these
promised gospel-blessings would involve the creation of 'one
new man' (Eph. 2. 15) by the incorporation of Jewish and Gentile
believers alike, on the common ground of divine grace, as fellow-
members of the body of Christ; and this is the mystery which
Paul unfolds in the following verse. The 'holy apostles and prophets' to whom God had now revealed this truth by the Spirit's
illumination are (as in 2. 20 and 4. 11) those of the first Christian
generation, of whom Paul was one—an apostle and prophet both.
But the proclamation of this mystery, and the ministry by which
it was to be fulfilled effectively, were committed pre-eminently
to him.

The reference to the 'holy apostles and prophets' has been felt
to have an impersonal ring about it which makes it difficult to
imagine Paul himself as writing it. But the difficulty lies rather
in our twentieth-century English ears than in the first-century

Greek of the New Testament: there is nothing formal or litur-
gical about Paul's use of the adjective 'holy', and nothing unnatural about the way in which he associates other apostles and
prophets with himself.

V. 6 *to wit*, **that the Gentiles are fellow-heirs, and fellow-
members of the body, and fellow-partakers of the promise
in Christ Jesus through the gospel,**—In these words the
mystery is summed up: it was God's eternal purpose, Paul says,
that the Gentiles should be joint-heirs (Gk. *synklēronomos*) of
an inheritance on which they had no claim by birth; 'concorporate'
(Gk. *syssōmos*, a Pauline coinage) with their brethren of Jewish
origin in the living unity of the body of Christ; joint-sharers (Gk.
symmetochos, cf. 5. 7) in those covenant-promises from which
they had once been excluded (Eph. 2. 12).[1] And these unlooked-
for privileges which God designed for them in ages past have now
been made good to them 'in Christ Jesus through the gospel'.

V. 7 **whereof I was made a minister, according to the
gift of that grace of God which was given me according to
the working of his power.**—Compare the last clause of Col. 1.
23, 'the hope of the gospel, . . . whereof I Paul was made a
minister'.[2] There as here 'whereof' means 'of the gospel'; but
here Paul is thinking especially of his stewardship of the mystery
just unfolded. All God's servants have gifts differing according
to the grace given to them (Rom. 12. 6); but Paul glorified his
personal ministry as an apostle of Gentiles (Rom. 11. 13). That
he of all people should be chosen for this service was to him a
matter for unending wonder and praise; it was a manifest token
of the working of God's power—and he uses language similar

---

[1] Paul's fondness for compounds with the prefix *syn* (cf. Eph. 2. 5 f., 19)
may be connected with his conception of Christians as fellow-members of the
body of Christ. His colleagues, too, are variously designated by means of such
compounds as his fellow-workers, fellow-servants, fellow-soldiers, fellow-
prisoners and the like. 'The dearest of all ties for Paul is to find men sharing
things with him. The work, the "athletic" life, the yoke, the slavery, the
imitation—these are all expressions of his relation with Jesus Christ, the very
essence of life; how much more it is to him when he finds his friends standing
with him in that great loyalty' (T. R. Glover, *Paul of Tarsus* (London, 1925),
p. 180).

[2] The clause is repeated at the beginning of Col. 1. 25 ('whereof I was made
a minister'), where the antecedent, however, is not 'the gospel' but 'the church'.

to that which he used in Eph. 1. 19 f. when he spoke of the display of God's power in the raising of Christ from the dead. And rightly so; it was that resurrection-power working in Paul that enabled him to accomplish what he did in bringing God's gracious purpose to fruition among the Gentiles.

5b. *Paul's Stewardship of the Mystery* (3. 8-13)

V. 8 Unto me, who am less than the least of all saints, was this grace given, to preach unto the Gentiles the unsearchable riches of Christ;—That Paul of all people should have been chosen as chief steward of the mystery of Christ was something which made him marvel the more, the more he thought about it. In an earlier epistle he had called himself 'the least of the apostles, . . . not meet to be called an apostle' (1 Cor. 15. 9); but here he takes a still lower place in his own estimation, and is well on the way to the language of 1 Tim. 1. 15—'sinners; of whom I am chief'. A recent writer, in ascribing the authorship of Ephesians to a disciple of Paul's rather than to the apostle himself, suggests that the present phrase was modelled on that of 1 Cor. 15. 9, and feels that 'in this new context the words have lost their original, direct simplicity, and even sound, in their artificial exaggeration, somewhat self-conscious and affected'.[1] We must express profound disagreement with this judgment; to us the words are a very hallmark of apostolic authenticity. No disciple of Paul's would have dreamed of giving the apostle so low a place. The word used for 'less than the least' (Gk. *elachistoteros*) is a comparative and superlative in one, perhaps coined by Paul himself (as some have thought) with a playful reference to the meaning of his own name (Latin *paullus*, 'little'). The adjective 'unsearchable' (Gk. *anexichniastos*) was used by Paul in Rom. 11. 33 of the ways of God in His dealings with Jews and

---

[1] C. L. Mitton, *The Epistle to the Ephesians* (Oxford, 1951), pp. 15, 136; he quotes with approval from E. J. Goodspeed's *Introduction to the New Testament*, p. 231, 'It gives scholars who maintain that Paul wrote it great embarrassment'. But one may consult commentary after commentary on this passage without finding any trace of embarrassment. In any case, no conclusive argument can be based on language which makes such totally different impressions on different readers.

Gentiles; its use here of the wealth of Christ's redeeming grace, lavished in the gospel upon Gentiles as well as Jews, is specially appropriate.

V. 9 **and to make all men see what is the dispensation of the mystery which from all ages hath been hid in God who created all things**;—'To make all men see' is literally 'to enlighten (Gk. *phōtizō*) all men'. Some good ancient authorities for the text omit 'all men'; the resultant reading is that rendered in the R.V. margin: 'to bring to light what is the dispensation of the mystery'. But the authority for retaining 'all men' is weightier. The 'dispensation of the mystery' which is thus to be brought to light throughout the world is the content of Paul's special stewardship, which he has already specified in verse 6. This 'mystery' which Paul has been charged to reveal in word and action was something which God had purposed and cherished from all eternity, until it was unfolded in the fulness of time. The use of the title 'God who created all things' reminds us not only that He is the One who fashions everything in accordance with His sovereign decrees, but also that it was before all creation that He chose His people in Christ (Eph. 1. 4). The additional phrase in A.V., 'by Jesus Christ', has poor attestation, as has also the reading 'fellowship' (Gk. *koinōnia*) for R.V. 'dispensation' (Gk. *oikonomia*).

V. 10 **to the intent that now unto the principalities and the powers in the heavenly** *places* **might be made known through the church the manifold wisdom of God,**—The accomplishment of this eternal purpose of God's has not in view only those who enter into the good of it on this earth. The triumph of His grace in overcoming an otherwise insurmountable barrier and uniting the two sections of mankind in Christ holds instruction for the inhabitants of the celestial realms. While the material universe presents ample evidence of the wisdom of God, the Church of the new creation (Eph. 2. 10) is the masterpiece of His wisdom—His diversified, 'many-coloured' wisdom, as Paul calls it, using a rare poetical adjective (Gk. *polypoikilos*). The principalities and powers, before whom this object-lesson of divine wisdom is displayed, probably include good and evil beings alike. In Colossians, for the most part (owing no doubt to the character of the Colossian heresy), as in Eph. 6. 12, the expression denotes supernatural forces opposed to God. The fact that God uses the church as a means of instructing the denizens of the heavenly places may throw light on 1 Cor. 11. 10, with its enigmatic phrase 'because of the angels'.[1]

V. 11 **according to the eternal purpose which he purposed in Christ Jesus our Lord**:—We who by faith are united with Christ and incorporated in Him are caught up in a divine purpose which spans eternity—'the purpose of the ages', as it is literally rendered (cf. R.V. margin). And the One to whom we are thus united is Himself the centre and circumference of this purpose: it was conceived (literally 'made') in Him and it attains its fulfilment through Him.

V. 12 **in whom we have boldness and access in confidence through our faith in him.**—If the One through whom, as Paul has already said (Eph. 2. 18), we have access to the Father is the One in whom God's eternal purpose is bound up, then our coming into the presence of God may be marked by the fullest confidence. 'Boldness', here as in 6. 19[2] (cf. Heb. 4. 16; 10. 19), is a rendering of Gk. *parrhēsia*, a word which normally denotes freedom of utterance or 'plainness of speech' (e.g. in 2 Cor. 3. 12). In classical Greek it signified the free speech which was the right of every citizen of a democratic state; when the word is 'baptized into Christ' it betokens the liberty of Christian men to approach God directly with no intermediary apart from Christ, who embraces Godhead and Manhood in His one person. The word translated 'confidence' (Gk. *pepoithēsis*) is a rare word, used in the New Testament by Paul only (six times). 'Our faith in him' is literally 'the faith of him' (so A.V.); but the genitive 'of him' is objective, denoting the One in whom the faith is placed.

---

[1] The implication of this phrase in 1 Cor. 11. 10 is probably that the unseen presence of angels in Christian gatherings calls for propriety in dress and demeanour. This interpretation is now supported by one or two similar expressions in the Qumran literature. (Cf. p. 32, n. 1; p. 106, n. 1.)

[2] So in Eph. 6. 20 'speak boldly' renders the cognate verb *parrhēsiazomai* (see p. 134).

5

V. 13 Wherefore I ask that ye faint not at my tribulations for you, which are your glory.—Paul is not much concerned lest he himself should faint or grow weary through his tribulations —although his language could conceivably be translated to that effect, as noticed in R.V. margin. He himself knew too well the One whom he had believed. But his friends and converts might be tempted to think that, if Paul were really in the path of God's will, he would not have so many trials to endure. Paul therefore tries to convey to them his own assurance that his tribulations are the direct consequence and a certain token of his obedience to God's eternal purpose. Since that purpose includes the blessing of the Gentiles, the hardships which befall Paul in the course of his ministry are hardships which he suffers for them (cf. Eph. 3. 1). If they can be brought to appreciate that, far from finding cause for discouragement in the spectacle of Paul's sufferings, they will glory in them as he himself had learned to do, seeing in them the proof that God's purpose was advancing towards its consummation. In Col. 1. 24 Paul regards his own sufferings as something which he is called upon to endure for the sake of the Church, the body of Christ, and as his filling up of 'that which is lacking of the afflictions of Christ'. That the sufferings of Christ's people are Christ's own sufferings Paul had learned on the Damascus road; now it is his desire to absorb as much as possible of these sufferings in his own person.[1]

6. THE PRAYER FOR WISDOM CONCLUDED (3. 14-19)

V. 14 For this cause I bow my knees unto the Father,— Paul's prayer for the impartation of heavenly wisdom to his readers, begun in Eph. 1. 15 ff., and then resumed in 3. 1, is now brought to its conclusion. The shorter reading 'the Father' is to be preferred here to the longer form found in A.V., 'the Father of our Lord Jesus Christ'. The amplification of the

---

[1] E. Best takes the sufferings of Col. 1. 24 as the messianic birth-pangs which had to be completed before Messiah's coming in glory; Paul will hasten that advent by exhausting these pangs himself (*One Body in Christ*, pp. 130 ff.). On Paul's eschatological understanding of his apostleship see J. Munck, *Paul and the Salvation of Mankind* (London, 1959), pp. 36 ff.

names and titles of Divine Persons is frequently a mark of later forms of the text as against earlier ones. But the simple title 'the Father' here accords better with the words which follow.

V. 15 **from whom every family in heaven and on earth is named,**—In translating Gk. *patria* by 'family' here, R.V. obscures for English readers the close association of this word with *patēr* ('Father') at the end of the preceding verse. R.V. margin makes the point with its more literal rendering 'fatherhood'. 'I bow my knees', says Paul, 'to the Father after whom all fatherhood takes its name'. That is to say, every species of fatherhood in the universe is derived from the original, archetypal Fatherhood of God: His is the only underived fatherhood. And the more nearly any fatherhood, natural or spiritual, approaches in character to God's perfect Fatherhood, the more truly does it manifest fatherhood as God intended it to be. (A.V., 'the whole family', would normally require the presence of the definite article in the Greek, but it is absent.)

V. 16 **that he would grant you, according to the riches of his glory, that ye may be strengthened with power through his Spirit in the inward man;**—Again the apostle proceeds to pile synonyms for power one upon another (cf. Eph. 1. 19) so as to emphasize the fulness of the divine knowledge which he craves on his readers' behalf. The verb 'be strengthened' is *krataioomai*; the noun translated 'power' is *dynamis*. This enabling, measured by the riches of God's glory (cf. 'the riches of his grace' in 1. 7), is the work of the Spirit; these people need to be strengthened in order to receive all the blessings that Paul seeks on their behalf, as a starving man needs to be strengthened in order to receive strong meat. 'The inward man' is the true and enduring self, which delights in the law of God (Rom. 7. 22) and experiences daily renewal in Christ however much the outward man may waste away (2 Cor. 4. 16).

V. 17 **that Christ may dwell in your hearts through faith;** —the tense of the verb 'dwell' is aorist; the words might therefore be rendered: 'that Christ may take up His abode in your hearts'. A striking parallel to this is found in John 14. 23, where our Lord says to Judas (not Iscariot): 'If a man love me, he will keep my word: and my Father will love him, and we will come unto him, and make our abode with him'.[1] The verbal expression used is different, but the meaning is similar. The faith of our present passage and the love of John 14. 23 are inseparable companions; we may compare the emphasis on love in the clause immediately following this.

to the end that ye, being rooted and grounded in love,— Here, as in Eph. 2. 21, biological and architectural figures are conjoined; plants are rooted, while buildings are founded (for that is the proper sense of the verb *themelioō*, here rendered 'grounded'). There is a noteworthy parallelism between this passage and Eph. 2. 19-22 in the recurrent references to 'dwelling' and 'founding'.[2] The two passages are closely connected by 'For this cause' in Eph. 3. 1, 14 (verses 2-13 being a parenthesis). A habitation of God in the Spirit must grow out of a rock-foundation of love. We may compare the expressions 'grounded and stedfast' in Col. 1. 23, and 'rooted and builded up . . . and stablished' in Col. 2. 7; a different figure is used in Col. 2. 2, 'knit together in love'.

V. 18 may be strong to apprehend with all the saints what is the breadth and length and height and depth,— Only by a supernatural enablement can Paul's readers realize the divine apprehension and infilling which he prays may be theirs. Nor should the implication of the phrase 'with all the saints' be overlooked. It is a vain thing for Christian individuals or groups to imagine that they can better attain to the fulness of spiritual maturity if they isolate themselves from their fellow-believers. Compare Eph. 4. 13: 'till we *all* attain . . . unto a fullgrown man'. But what is the object which they are to apprehend with all the saints—the object whose fourfold dimensions are specified by the apostle? Probably it is the *plērōma* or 'fulness' of God (cf. the exposition of Eph. 1. 23). But how can

---

[1] Cf. Rev. 3. 20.
[2] I am indebted to Mr. Andrew Borland for drawing my attention to this parallelism.

human beings, finite creatures still, for all their endowment with spiritual blessings in the heavenly realm in Christ, ever hope to apprehend that which is infinite and eternal? Only in so far as that which is infinite and eternal has condescended to their estate and capacity. And He in whom 'dwelleth all the fulness of the Godhead bodily' (Col. 2. 9) has in love declared to us the infinite God whom no man has seen at any time (John 1. 18; 1 John 4. 12). Hence Paul conjoins apprehension of the 'breadth and length and depth and height' with knowing the love of Christ.

V. 19 **and to know the love of Christ which passeth knowledge,**—To know what transcends knowledge is paradox enough, but what is impossible for us in ourselves becomes an experienced reality in Christ, for those who are seated with Him in the heavenly places. There, a knowledge from which the highest angels are shut out is granted to sinners saved by grace.

> Stronger His love than death or hell,
> Its riches are unsearchable:
>   The firstborn sons of light
> Desire in vain its depths to see;
> They cannot reach the mystery,
>   The length, and breadth, and height.

that ye may be filled unto all the fulness of God.—There is no limit to the spiritual infilling which Paul seeks on behalf of his readers, short of the fulness of God Himself. He does not simply pray, as A.V. and R.S.V. put it, that they may 'be filled with all the fulness of God'; the preposition 'unto' (Gk. *eis*) suggests rather their being progressively filled 'up to the measure of' God's fulness, just as in Eph. 4. 13 he speaks of their ultimately reaching 'the measure of the stature of the fulness of Christ'. Only in Christ can the apostle's prayer be answered; in Christ the divine fulness is ideally theirs already, but his earnest desire is that it may increasingly be realized in their experience. In Col. 2. 19 he dwells upon the process, increasing 'with the increase of God'; here he dwells upon the consummation. 'Filled unto all the fulness of God'—nothing can exceed this; here every other blessing is comprehended and crowned.

7. A Doxology (3. 20-21)

V. 20 **Now unto him that is able to do exceeding abundantly above all that we ask or think,**—The apostle's far-ranging prayer for his fellow-Christians concludes with a spontaneous outburst of praise. Has he asked for too much—that they should know Christ's knowledge-surpassing love, that they should be filled up to the measure of God's own fulness? No, indeed! However far the desire or thought of man can reach—even the desire and thought of an apostle in such an exalted moment of inspiration—God is able to do infinitely more. Paul coins one of his super-superlatives to express the 'exceeding abundance' of God's capacity to transcend all that we ask or think—*hyperekperissou*, 'superabundantly'.

according to the power that worketh in us,—This power is, of course, the power of God operating in His people, and no natural energy of theirs. Paul had already prayed that his readers might be enabled by God to know 'the exceeding greatness of His power to us-ward who believe, according to that working of the strength of His might which He wrought in Christ, when He raised Him from the dead, and made Him to sit at His right hand in the heavenly places' (Eph. 1. 19 f.). And it is by no lesser power than this that God acts in those who are united to Christ, 'both to will and to work, for His good pleasure' (Phil. 2. 13).

V. 21 **unto him** *be* **the glory in the church and in Christ Jesus**—The Western text reverses the order, so as to read 'in Christ Jesus and in the church'; some later uncials omit 'and', thus yielding the A.V. reading, 'in the church by Christ Jesus'. But the best authenticated reading presents an ascending order of worth: in the Church, which is the body of Christ, and in Christ Jesus, who is Head of His Church, let God be glorified. In the heavenly places, where the people of Christ are raised with Him in the purpose of God to share His enthronement at God's right hand, God is indeed glorified. But here upon earth, where the people of Christ live in mortal body, God may be glorified, too; and how this may be accomplished is unfolded in the second half of our epistle.

unto all generations for ever and ever. Amen.—Again, Paul piles synonym on synonym to emphasize the eternity of God's praise: 'unto all the generations of the age of the ages' (as R.V. margin renders it literally). Since it is God's will 'in the ages to come' to display the 'exceeding riches of His grace' in those who have been its most signal beneficiaries, so throughout these coming ages, one age supervening upon another into the remotest infinity, it is that excelling grace of His which will redound to His highest glory. Well may the apostle add his 'Amen'; but it is not his 'Amen' alone, but the 'Amen' of the whole new creation. On this transcendent note the first part of the epistle ends.

> Praise to the Lord; O let all that is in me adore Him!
> All that hath life and breath, come now with praises before Him!
> Let the Amen
> Sound from His people again;
> Gladly for aye we adore Him.

PART II

THE NEW COMMUNITY IN THE LIFE OF BELIEVERS

(Chapters 4-6)

CHAPTER IV

1. UNITY IN DIVERSITY IN THE BODY OF CHRIST (4. 1-16)

V. 1 I therefore, the prisoner in the Lord, beseech you to walk worthily of the calling wherewith ye were called, —As in other epistles, Paul's transition from the doctrinal to the practical realm is marked by the word 'therefore' (cf. Rom. 12. 1; Col. 3. 5). Because the basic facts of our holy faith are such as have been set forth, Christians ought to live in accordance with them; their character and conduct should match their creed and confession. In this epistle, where Christians are taught the hope of their calling (Eph. 1. 18), Paul insists that their earthly behaviour should be worthy of that calling. Those who have been chosen by God to sit with Christ in the heavenly places must remember that the honour of Christ is involved in their daily lives. There are many situations in which we shall find no detailed precept of Scripture to tell us what to do, but here is a principle to guide us in every situation: which course of action will be most worthy of the calling with which God has called us? As in Eph. 3. 1, Paul adds to the weight of his exhortation by reminding his readers that he is 'the prisoner in the Lord'— enduring captivity for Christ's sake.

V. 2 with all lowliness and meekness, with longsuffering, forbearing one another in love;—Paul goes on to specify four graces the cultivation of which will produce a life worthy of the Christian calling. These are humility, gentleness, patience, and loving forbearance. Lowliness or humility was regarded as more of a vice than a virtue in pagan antiquity, although the Old Testament anticipated the Christian revelation by affirming repeatedly that God chooses the humble to be His companions (cf. Isa. 57. 15; 66. 2; Mic. 6. 8). It was the influence of One who was meek and lowly in heart, operating in His followers, that elevated a term which had formerly been despicable rather than praiseworthy. Meekness or gentleness is far from being an easygoing weakness; it is the property of a mind and spirit kept under due control. Mutual patience and forbearance are not graces which come readily or naturally; but those who have learned to appreciate gratefully God's patience and forbearance with them will desire to show the same attitude to others. Paul is, in effect, urging his readers to cultivate the graces that were seen in perfection in Christ, and to love one another as He had loved them.

V. 3 **giving diligence to keep the unity of the Spirit in the bond of peace.**—The unity spoken of here is the unity of heart which the Spirit of God fosters in a community of believers. The English word 'unity' (and the underlying Greek word *henotēs*) can have more than one meaning, and we should not interpret 'unity' here by relating it to the recurring 'one' of verses 4-6. In verses 4-6 it is uniqueness that is intended. The unity of the Spirit here is a different thing from the statement that there is 'one Spirit' in verse 4. The fact that there is one Spirit of God is something which cannot be affected by any endeavour or action of men one way or the other. But in the present passage Paul is inculcating the same mutual attitude as when in Phil. 2. 2 he exhorts the Philippian Christians to 'be of the same mind, having the same love, being of one accord, of one mind'. If that is so, then 'the unity of the Spirit' is best maintained when Christians have this mind in them 'which was also in Christ Jesus' (Phil. 2. 5). Or, to put it otherwise, when the graces commended in verse 2 are cultivated, the unity of the Spirit is preserved. The expression here bears practically the same meaning as 'the communion of the Holy Spirit' in 2 Cor. 13. 14. And those in whom the unity of the Spirit is displayed will be joined together 'in the bond of peace'. We may compare Col. 3. 14, where love is the perfect 'bond' (Gk. *syndesmos*, as here) which binds the other Christian graces together. God is the author of peace, and the sowing of 'discord among brethren' (the opposite of keeping the unity of the Spirit) is an abomination in His sight (cf. Prov. 6. 16, 19b).

V. 4 *There is* **one body, and one Spirit, even as also ye were called in one hope of your calling**;—Paul now introduces a sevenfold uniqueness, which is fundamental for Christian faith and life.

First, there is *one body*. That is, of course, the body of Christ, comprising all His people, which has already been mentioned in Eph. 1. 23 and 2. 16. Jewish and Gentile believers alike had been reconciled to God in this one body. To think, for example, of two bodies of Christ, one comprising Jewish believers and the other comprising Gentile believers, would be grotesque. So in Col. 3. 15 Paul reminds the Colossian Christians that they were called to the peace of Christ 'in one body'; fellow-members of one body must co-operate harmoniously.

Secondly, there is *one Spirit*. The Spirit who came down in power on Jewish believers at Pentecost is the same as fell on Gentile believers in the house of Cornelius. The correlation between the one Spirit and the one body is set out in fuller detail in 1 Cor. 12. 13: 'For in one Spirit were we all baptized into one body, whether Jews or Greeks, whether bond or free; and were all made to drink of one Spirit'. Just as the body is one, though its members are many, so the Spirit is one, though His gifts and operations are many.

Thirdly, there is *one hope*. The hope of our calling—the hope which God set before us when He called us by His grace—is the hope of sharing the glory of Christ. As members of His body, we share His resurrection life now; as those who are in-dwelt and led by His Spirit, we are to be increasingly conformed to His likeness now; but the consummation of what we now enjoy in part awaits the day when we shall be like Him because we shall see Him as He is (cf. 1 John 3. 2). And this one hope is set before all believers, all whom God has called according to His purpose. There is no distinction in this respect between those of Jewish and Gentile birth, neither is there any favoured *élite* within the believing community for whom better things are reserved than for the rank and file.

V. 5 **one Lord, one faith, one baptism,**—Fourthly, as Paul had said in an earlier epistle, 'to us there is . . . *one Lord*, Jesus Christ, through whom are all things, and we through him' (1 Cor. 8. 6). The acknowledgment of this one Lord was a matter of the most vital consequence to many Christians in the early centuries of our era. Because they had but one Lord, they refused to give the title 'Lord' to others who claimed it, notably to the Roman Emperor, when it was claimed in a sense that implied divinity. Of course the Greek *kyrios* or the Latin *dominus* could also be used as a courtesy title, like 'my lord' or 'sir' among us, and there was no objection to using it that way, but there was every objection to using it in a sense which meant that the unique Lordship of Christ was being infringed.

Fifthly, there is *one faith*. Faith may denote the act and attitude of believing, or it may mean the substance of one's belief. In both senses it is true that Christians have but one faith. It is true if we think of the one faith as the faith which they place in Christ as their Lord and Saviour; it is true if we think of it as 'the faith which was once for all delivered to the saints' (Jude 3). There is not one faith for Jews and another for Gentiles, since 'God is one, and he shall justify the circumcision by faith, and the uncircumcision through faith' (Rom. 3. 30)—one and the same faith in either case. A book on Christian doctrine appeared some time ago under the title, *No Faith of My Own*.[1] The author's intention in this title was to emphasize that the faith of which the book treated was no private system devised by himself but the common faith of all Christian people. In our present passage faith is probably to be understood subjectively of faith in Christ: there is one faith, since there is but one Lord.

Sixthly, there is *one baptism*. If this were not expressly stated here, many Christians when asked how many baptisms there are would probably answer: 'Two; baptism in water and the baptism of the Spirit'. But it should be noted that when water-baptism and Spirit-baptism are set in opposition in the New Testament, the water-baptism is John's baptism and not Christian baptism. When our Lord said, 'John indeed baptized with water; but ye shall be baptized with the Holy Spirit' (Acts 1. 5), He did not mean that water-baptism would be superseded by baptism with the Spirit. On the contrary, when the descent of the Spirit on the first Gentile believers reminded Peter of these words of his

---

[1] By J. V. L. Casserley (London, 1950).

Lord (Acts 11. 16), the first thing he did was to command these converts 'to be baptized in the name of Jesus Christ' (Acts 10. 48), and it is made quite plain that this was water-baptism. Water-baptism remains in force throughout the Christian age, although it has now received a richer significance from the saving work of Christ and the bestowal of the Holy Spirit. The baptism of the Spirit which it was our Lord's prerogative to impart took place primarily on the day of Pentecost when He poured forth 'the promise of the Father' on His disciples and thus constituted them the Spirit-baptized fellowship of the people of God. Baptism in water continued to be the outward and visible sign by which individuals who believed the gospel, repented of their sins, and acknowledged Jesus as Lord, were publicly incorporated into this Spirit-baptized fellowship—'baptized into Christ' (Gal. 3. 27). It must be remembered that in New Testament times repentance and faith, regeneration and conversion, baptism in water, reception of the Holy Spirit, incorporation into Christ, admission to church fellowship and first communion were all parts of a single complex of events which took place within a very short time, and not always in a uniform order. Logically they were distinguishable, but in practice they were all bound up with the transition from the old life to the new.[1] Consequently, what was logically true of one specific part of the complex experience might be predicated of the whole experience, or something that was more particularly applicable to one part might be transferred in speech or writing to another part. These considerations may help evangelical readers of the New Testament who feel uneasy when baptism or water is referred to as the instrument of regeneration, or of entering into membership of Christ's body.[2] It is, moreover, a natural use of language when a symbol is said to effect that which, in strict fact, it symbolizes. But the New Testament epistles were not addressed to theologians, accustomed to hair-

---

[1] There has been an abundant output of literature in recent years on this subject; two works which may be specially commended are G. W. H. Lampe, *The Seal of the Spirit* (London, 1951), and R. E. O. White, *The Biblical Doctrine of Initiation* (London, 1960).

[2] Cf. Eph. 5. 26 with the accompanying exposition (pp. 115 ff.).

splitting distinctions, but to very ordinary Christians, who would inevitably think of their own baptism in water when they read the word 'baptism', unless the context made it quite clear that another baptism was meant. If the 'one baptism' here had meant Spirit-baptism to the exclusion of water-baptism, it would surely have been associated with 'one Spirit' and not 'one Lord'. But the point here is that Jewish and Gentile believers alike acknowledged one Lord, shared one faith in Him, and had undergone one baptism into His name.[1]

V. 6 **one God and Father of all, who is over all, and through all, and in all.**—Seventhly, there is *one God and Father*. Here Paul echoes the language of an Old Testament prophet: 'Have we not all one father? hath not one God created us?' (Mal. 3. 10). But thanks to the Son of God, who came to show us the way to the Father and to show us the Father Himself, our appreciation of the Fatherhood of God is deeper than it could have been before Christ came. Now Gentiles as well as Jews have come through Christ to know this one God as their Father. It was to former pagans, worshippers of many gods, that Paul wrote in 1 Cor. 8. 6: 'Yet to us there is one God, the Father; of whom are all things, and we unto him'. He is the Creator of all and the goal of all; transcendent over all, pervasive throughout all, immanent in all. The second-century heretic Marcion, and his imitators in following centuries, might try to distinguish between the Old Testament God who created the world and the New Testament God whom Jesus revealed as the Father; but neither Paul nor any other biblical writer knows of such a distinction. The Father of our Lord Jesus Christ, who has accepted us for Christ's sake and listens to our prayers, is 'the everlasting God, the Lord, the Creator of the ends of the earth' (Isa. 40. 28), 'one God and Father of all'.

In these three verses (4-6) Paul is very probably quoting and amplifying a primitive confession of faith. The acknowledgement

---

[1] It is a special pleasure to refer, for a fuller treatment of this important subject, to seven papers on 'Baptism in Ephesians' which appeared in the editorial pages of successive issues of *The Believer's Magazine* between March and September, 1954.

of 'one Spirit, . . . one Lord, . . . one God and Father . . .' reminds us how thoroughly apostolic the doctrine of the Trinity is. We may compare the mention of 'the same Spirit . . . the same Lord . . . the same God' in 1 Cor. 12. 4-6. Let us not be misled by the foolish argument that because the term 'Trinity' does not occur in the Scriptures, the doctrine of the Trinity is therefore unscriptural. The classical formulations of the doctrine are later than the apostolic age, but the doctrine which they formulate is thoroughly apostolic. It is round such confessions of faith in the triune Godhead that the historic creeds of the Church have been constructed. Those creeds which come from the East retain the word 'one' in a way that suggests dependence on this passage in Ephesians (or the primitive confession which it reproduces); the Palestinian creeds, for example, which formed the basis for the creed of Nicaea (A.D. 325), were built up around the three clauses: 'We believe in one God the Father Almighty . . . and in one Lord Jesus Christ . . . and in one Holy Spirit'.[1]

V. 7 **But unto each one of us was the grace given according to the measure of the gift of Christ.**—Alongside the sevenfold uniqueness of the preceding verses Paul now introduces the variety of the gifts bestowed on the Church. As he had already written in 1 Cor. 12. 4, 'there are diversities of gifts, but the same Spirit'. Whereas the gifts are spoken of in 1 Cor. 12 as gifts of the Spirit, they are spoken of here as gifts of the exalted Christ. There is, of course, no essential contradiction in this: the Holy Spirit Himself is given by the exalted Christ to His Church (Acts 2. 33), and so the gifts of the Spirit may also be thought of as gifts of the exalted Christ. The grace which each believer has received for the discharge of his particular function in the community is proportionate to the gift which he has freely received from his glorified Lord.

V. 8   **Wherefore he saith,**
     When he ascended on high,
     he led captivity captive,
     And gave gifts unto men.—

---

[1] Cf. Eph. 2. 18 with accompanying exposition (pp. 55 f.).

In this bestowal of gifts by the ascended Christ, Paul finds the fulfilment of an Old Testament passage (Psa. 68. 18) which (significantly enough) was associated in the synagogue calendar with Pentecost. He introduces his quotation with a phrase which may mean either 'Wherefore He (i.e. God) saith' or 'Wherefore it (i.e. Scripture) saith'. In practice it makes no difference; such expressions as 'God says', 'Scripture says' and 'it says' are used indiscriminately in the New Testament where the Old Testament is being quoted. As Paul quotes the passage, there is one note-worthy divergence from the Hebrew and Septuagint texts. Where they read 'Thou hast *received* gifts *among* men,' he quotes the form 'He . . . *gave* gifts *unto* men'. This reading is also attested in Jewish antiquity; it found its way into the Syriac version of the Old Testament (the Peshitta) and into the Targum or Aramaic paraphrase of the Psalter.[1] The original picture is of a victorious king ascending the mountain of the Lord in triumphal procession, attended by a long train of captives, receiving tribute from his new subjects (according to the one reading) and bestowing largesse upon the crowds which line his processional route (according to the other reading). For Paul's present purpose the reading which speaks of the conqueror as *giving* gifts is more appropriate than that which speaks of him as *receiving* them; but if this secondary reading had not been available to him the first would not have been unsuitable; the ascended Christ may well be pictured as receiving from His Father the gifts which He proceeds to bestow among men. Very reasonably, however, Paul selects from the two alternative readings the one which best fits his immediate context. And after quoting the text, he gives an exposition of the salient words. He does not relate the clause 'he led captivity captive' to his present argument; if he had done so, we may infer which line he would have followed from Col. 2. 15, where Christ turns His cross into a triumphal chariot, before which He drives the vanquished principalities and powers whose

---

[1] In the Targum the passage is interpreted of Moses' ascent of Mount Sinai to receive the law which he then delivered to Israel; in later Judaism Pentecost was regarded as the anniversary of the law-giving.

attack upon Him has been so signally frustrated.[1] There is
little basis for the traditional view that the reference is to the
harrowing of hell—that the captivity which He led captive con-
sists here of the souls of men whom His victory liberated from the
thraldom of death.

V. 9 (**Now this, He ascended, what is it but that he also
descended into the lower parts of the earth?**—A number of
texts insert 'first' after 'descended' (thus making explicit what is
in any case implicit). Some texts also omit 'parts' (Gk. *merē*)
after 'lower' (Gk. *katōtera*), and this omission may well be
original; but so far as the English version is concerned a word
like 'parts' or 'places' is required to complete the sense. The
fact, says Paul, that the psalmist speaks of Christ as having
'ascended on high' implies that, before doing so, He must have
descended; and descend He did—into the lower regions of the
earth. But what exactly are these lower regions? Three alternative interpretations may be mentioned. First, the reference
may be to Hades (the Old Testament *Sheol*), the abode of the
dead; in Scripture this is regularly a region to which one goes
down from the earth's surface. So, in Acts 2. 25-35, the fact that
Christ (in fulfilment of Psa. 16. 10) was not left in Hades is the
correlative of His being exalted to God's right hand (in fulfilment
of Psa. 110. 1). Secondly, the reference may be to the sepulchre
in which His body was laid. Thirdly, the phrase 'of the earth'
may be construed as a genitive of definition, in which case the
lower regions are themselves the earth, to which He came down
from heaven and from which He was raised to His present place
of glory. A comparison with Rom. 10. 6 f., where ascending into
heaven is contrasted with descending 'into the abyss (that is, to
bring Christ up from the dead)', suggests that the first of these
three alternatives is the true interpretation here. We may also
compare Phil. 2. 8 f., where it is from the lowest depths of death
that Christ is 'highly exalted' by the Father. So, Paul seems to
say here, Christ descended from heaven not merely to earth but

---

[1] Cf. 1 Cor. 2. 8; also Eph. 6. 12 and accompanying exposition (pp. 127 f.).

to Hades, and from Hades He has ascended again 'far above all
the heavens'.

V. 10 **He that descended is the same also that ascended
far above all the heavens, that he might fill all things.)**—
Christ's exaltation to the place of highest supremacy has been
emphasized by Paul in Eph. 1. 20, 23. In our present passage
the purpose of His exaltation is said to be 'that he might fill all
things'—that is to say, that He might pervade the whole universe
with His presence, from the lowest depths to the highest heights.
This, as we have seen, corresponds with a possible (though not
perhaps the most probable) meaning of the clause 'that filleth all
in all' in Eph. 1. 23. At any rate, He who already embodies the
fulness of the Godhead (Col. 2. 9) is the one who now fills the
universe. That is why His people can now enjoy His immediate
presence simultaneously, wherever they may be,[1] whereas in the
days of His flesh He could only be in one place at one time.

V. 11 **And he gave some** *to be* **apostles; and some, prophets; and some evangelists; and some, pastors and
teachers;**—In 1 Cor. 12. 4 ff. the gifts of the Spirit are endow-
ments bestowed by Him upon individual Christians, which they
are expected to exercise in the Church. Here the gifts of the
ascended Christ are the individual Christians who are thus endowed, bestowed by Him upon the Church. The substance of
this verse is paralleled in 1 Cor. 12. 28 ('And God hath set some
in the church, first apostles, secondly prophets, thirdly teachers
. . .'), although there the apostles, prophets and teachers are
not expressly called 'gifts'; they are rather thought of as men who
have received the respective gifts of apostleship, prophecy,
teaching and so forth. An honourable status indeed is conferred
on those who exercise their special ministries in the Church when
they are presented to the Church as gifts imparted to her by her
exalted Lord.

The first two gifts are 'apostles' and 'prophets', both these

---

[1] Thus receiving the fulfilment of such words as Matt. 18. 20 ('where two or
three are gathered together in my name, there am I in the midst of them')
and 28. 20 ('lo, I am with you alway, even unto the end of the world').

terms to be understood in the sense which they bear in Eph. 2. 20 and 3. 5. In our note on Eph. 2. 20 it was suggested that the 'foundation of the apostles and prophets' there is a reference to the apostles and prophets of the first Christian generation, who formed the Lord's foundation-gifts to His Church. Paul used the term 'apostles' in two main senses: (i) of those who were immediately commissioned by Christ to preach the gospel; (ii) of others who, though not immediately commissioned by Christ as Paul and the Jerusalem apostles were, preached the gospel in close association with those who were apostles in the stricter sense (so in 1 Thess. 2. 6 he links Timothy and Silvanus with himself as 'apostles of Christ').[1] The prophets of the apostolic age were men who from time to time spoke in the churches under the direct prompting of the Spirit of God (cf. Acts 11. 27 ff.; 13. 1 ff.; 21. 4, 9; 1 Cor. 14. 1 ff.). Toward the end of the apostolic age it became increasingly necessary to test the claims of these people, to see whether they spoke by the inspiration of the Spirit of God or of a very different kind of spirit (1 John 4. 1 ff.; Rev. 2. 20).[2] In the churches of the first generation the apostles and prophets discharged a unique rôle, which in some essential features has been taken over by the canonical writings of the New Testament.

The second pair of gifts, evangelists and pastor-teachers (or teaching pastors), are required in each generation. The Church can never dispense with men who preach the gospel and bring men and women to the knowledge of the truth, nor yet with men who can teach and guide in the way of truth those who have been evangelized and converted. The two terms 'pastors (shepherds) and teachers' denote one and the same class of men. They are the men who 'tend the flock of God' and care for its wellbeing, showing other Christians by precept and example alike the path of Christian faith and life (1 Pet. 5. 2; Acts 20. 28). They are the same people as are elsewhere called elders and bishops, one

---

[1] For the more general sense of the word as applied to 'messengers of the churches', see the exposition of Eph. 1. 1 (p. 25).
[2] How the test was applied in the post-apostolic age may be seen from the eastern manual of church order called the *Didache*; cf. F. F. Bruce, *The Spreading Flame* (London, 1958), pp. 214 ff.

of whose qualifications is being 'apt to teach' (1 Tim. 3. 2).

V. 12 **for the perfecting of the saints, unto the work of ministering, unto the building up of the body of Christ:—** The gifts mentioned are not the only ones bestowed by Christ upon the Church; but these are of the first importance. And their purpose is 'to equip the saints for work of service, for building up of the body of Christ'.[1] This rendering of the verse is supported by the fact that there is a change of preposition in the verse, indicated by a corresponding change in R.V., from 'for' (*eis*) to 'unto' (*pros*). That is to say, the gifts enumerated in verse 11 do not monopolize the Church's ministry; their function rather is so to help and direct the Church that all the members may perform their several ministries for the good of the whole. 'In the theocracy of grace there is in fact no laity' (E. K. Simpson). The word *katartismos*, rendered 'perfecting', denotes adjustment or equipment; the verb *katartizō*, from which it is derived, has a wide and interesting range of meaning in the New Testament.[2] As Paul uses the biological verb 'growth' in Eph. 2. 21 in a context where the building figure is being used of the Church, so here he uses the term 'building up' in a context where the figure of the body is being used. The healthy growth of the believing community is the aim in view in all the ministries which the Lord has entrusted to His people.

V. 13 **till we all attain unto the unity of the faith, and of the knowledge of the Son of God, unto a full-grown man, unto the measure of the stature of the fulness of Christ:—** This 'unity of the faith' is not so much the fact that there is 'one faith' (emphasized in verse 5) as the unity among believers which is produced by their common sharing of 'the knowledge of the Son of God'. Each individual Christian ought to grow up into spiritual maturity, but spiritual maturity in the individual Christian is not enough: there must be spiritual maturity in the cor-

---

[1] For this rendering see W. F. Arndt and F. W. Gingrich, *Greek-English Lexicon of the New Testament* (Cambridge, 1956), p. 419, under *katartismos*, the Greek word here rendered 'perfecting' in R.V.

[2] Cf. W. E. Vine, *Expository Dictionary of New Testament Words*, Vol. III (London, 1940), pp. 174 f., under *perfect*, B.3.

porate personality of the church. And one indispensable prere-
quisite for such corporate maturity is spiritual unity. Paul has already spoken of 'the unity of the Spirit' in verse 3, and it is no
different unity that he has in mind here, although he describes it in
terms which draw attention to some of its outstanding features.
The 'unity of the faith' to which he desires his readers to attain,
along with himself, depends not simply on the initial act of faith by
which one enters into the family of God, but on that ever-increas-
ing appreciation of all that is involved in Christian faith for living
and thinking. And this appreciation is best reached in fellowship
with one another. His words, 'till we all attain', remind us of his
language in Eph. 3. 18, where he prays that his readers 'may be
strong to apprehend with all the saints' the many-dimensioned
fulness of Christ. The higher reaches of the Christian life cannot
be attained in isolation from one's fellow-believers. The 'knowledge of the Son of God' which is a further feature of this unity
is not so much a mental comprehension of the doctrine of Christ
as an increasing personal acquaintance with Him in corporate
as well as individual experience. A community of believers
which manifests this 'unity of the faith, and of the knowledge
of the Son of God' is a mature church, in which the doctrine
of the body of Christ is not merely honoured in word but
exhibited in deed as a living reality. What is stated as the goal
for the Church Universal can be sought and attained here and
now in particular local churches. The Greek word *hēlikia*,
translated 'stature' here, may be used not only of height (as
in Luke 19. 3, where Zacchaeus is 'little of *stature*') but also
of age (as in John 9. 21, where 'he is of age' is literally 'he has
hēlikia').[1] The Church is already the fulness of Christ by
the call of God (Eph. 1. 23); now she is to attain that fulness in
the spiritual growth and life of her members. When the goal is
ultimately reached, and the body of Christ has grown up sufficiently

---

[1] Which of the two senses should be understood in Matt. 6. 27 and Luke 12.
25 is an unresolved question. Does our Lord mean that anxiety will not prolong
a man's life or that it will not increase his stature? (In both places R.V. text has
'stature' for *hēlikia*, while the margin gives 'age'; the word rendered 'cubit' can
be used as a unit of time as well as linear measurement.)

to match the Head Himself, then will be seen that full-grown Man which is Christ together with His members. That spectacle will not fully appear until the day when they are glorified together with Him; but the expectation of that day will act as a powerful incentive to spiritual development in the present time.

V. 14 **that we may be no longer children, tossed to and fro and carried about with every wind of doctrine, by the sleight of men, in craftiness, after the wiles of error**;— With maturity comes a stability born of spiritual experience. Some Christians attain it quite early; others never attain it, but to the end of their days run eagerly after the latest religious fashion, the 'wind of doctrine' that happens to be blowing most strongly at the time. They fall an easy prey to the specious sophistries of religious propagandists, for they have never learned to recognize the standard by which all religious teaching must be judged, or else they recognize it only in theory, but have never learned to make use of it. Therefore they are taken in 'by the cunning of men, by their craftiness in deceitful wiles' (R.S.V.). The word translated 'sleight' (Gk. *kybeia*) is borrowed from dice-games; 'craftiness' (*panourgia*) denotes the rascality that sticks at nothing to gain its ends; the phrase 'wiles of error' (*methodia tēs planēs*) indicates deceptive stratagems of various kinds. One particular 'wind of doctrine' which Paul probably had in mind was the incipient Gnosticism against which he had recently warned the Colossian church: 'Take heed lest there shall be any one that maketh spoil of you through his philosophy and vain deceit, after the tradition of men, after the rudiments of the world, and not after Christ' (Col. 2. 8). And the number of such attractive perversions of the gospel has not grown less in the interval that separates apostolic days from ours.

V. 15 **but speaking truth in love, may grow up in all things into him, which is the head,** *even* **Christ**;—The verb *alētheuō* in this context probably means not only *speaking* truth but living and acting it as well—'dealing truly', as R.V. margin puts it. Such true dealing is the very antithesis of the roguery described by the apostle in the preceding verse. Those who blindly follow the ways of error come to spiritual disaster; those who accept the truth become men of truth themselves. And gospel truth is never unaccompanied by love. We hear of some people who are 'all truth and no love', but in fact people without love cannot be 'all truth', any more than people without a concern for truth can be 'all love' in any serious sense of the term. 'Grace and truth came by Jesus Christ' (John 1. 17), and something of the same balance between these qualities should characterize His followers too. The epistle which affirms that 'God is love' also affirms that 'God is light, and in Him is no darkness at all' (1 John 4. 8, 16; 1. 5); and from this it draws the corollary that the children of God should 'abide in love' and 'walk in light' (1 John 4. 16; 1. 7).

It is, however, possible to punctuate the sentence so as to take 'in love' along with the words that follow. The importance of combining love with truth would not be diminished by so doing, but added emphasis would be laid on love as the means by which the people of Christ attain maturity, and there is much to be said for construing the passage thus, especially in the light of verse 16.

On the remarkable injunction to 'grow up into the head', Mgr. R. A. Knox pointed out that a baby's head is very large in relation to his body, and that his body, as it develops, is really growing up more and more into a due proportion with the head.[1] Whether this sort of analogy was in Paul's mind or not, it serves as a pleasing illustration of his teaching here. It is by growing up to match the Head that the body of Christ—the believing community—attains 'the measure of the stature of the fulness of Christ'.

V. 16 **from whom all the body fitly framed and knit together through that which every join supplieth, according to the working in** *due* **measure of each several part, maketh the increase of the body unto the building up of itself in love.**—Each part of the body will function as it ought while it is under the control of the head; if it escapes from this control and

---

[1] *Saint Paul's Gospel* (London, 1953), p. 84.

tries to act independently, the result is very distressing. So it is under the control of Christ that the members of His Church function harmoniously together, sharing His life and attaining maturity under His fostering care, supplied with nourishment and fitted together by means of the 'joints and ligaments' (cf. Col. 2. 19). The phrase 'fitly framed' is a rendering of the Greek verb *synarmologeō*, which we have already noted in Eph. 2. 21 (its only other New Testament occurrence), where it is used of the harmonious construction of the Church as 'a holy temple in the Lord'. The phrase 'knit together' represents Gk. *symbibazō* ('to put together'), which has this same sense in Col. 2. 2, 19. The word rendered 'joints' (Gk. *haphē*) probably denotes the ligaments by which the various parts of the body are connected. So Paul's desire is that his readers, 'living in accordance with the truth, may grow up in love altogether into Him who is the Head, even Christ, from whom the whole body, adjusted and fitted together by every ligament with which it is supplied, according to the harmonious functioning of each separate part, acquires the power to grow up as a perfect organism, so that it is built up in love'. The biological and architectural figures remain associated in his mind, as is plain from his speaking in one breath of 'growing up' and 'being built up'.

2. The Old Life and the New Contrasted
(4. 17-24)

V. 17 **This I say therefore, and testify in the Lord, that ye no longer walk as the Gentiles also walk,**—Paul harks back to verse 1, where he had besought his readers to 'walk worthily of the calling' with which they had been called. He now shows in detail the sort of thing he means. He emphasizes, too, that the following injunctions are not his own; in laying them down he is bearing witness with authority, as the apostle of the Lord, to those who belong to the same Lord. It is *the Lord's* will that they should cease to live the old pagan life. The word 'other', inserted before 'Gentiles' in later MSS. (cf. A.V.), is no part of the original text; Christians constitute a 'third race'[1] on earth, no longer Jews, no longer Gentiles (cf. 1 Cor. 10. 32). The 'also' of R.V. is a little misleading; it renders Gk. *kai*, which here serves simply to emphasize the adverbial conjunction 'as' ('as indeed the Gentiles walk' would bring out the sense better). How, then, do Gentile pagans live?

in the vanity of their mind,—So in Rom. 1. 21, in his grim portrayal of the pagan world, Paul says that in consequence of their failure to acknowledge God, men 'became vain in their reasonings'. Vanity in the New Testament is sometimes closely associated with idolatry, e.g. in Acts 14. 15, where the men of Lystra, on the point of offering idolatrous sacrifices, are urged to 'turn from these vain things unto the living God'.

V. 18 **being darkened in their understanding,**—Again we are reminded of Rom. 1. 21, 'their senseless heart was darkened'. How could it be otherwise, when men turn their backs upon the true Light?

alienated from the life of God because of the ignorance that is in them, because of the hardening of their heart; —The estrangement of mankind from God involves a state of spiritual death, for God, who is Himself life, is the only source of life for all His creatures. Conversely, the life which the believer receives as a gift from God is God's own life—*The Life of God in the Soul of Man*, to quote the title of Henry Scougall's classic work.[2] Paul ascribes this estrangement from God to men's innate ignorance, but an ignorance which is not excusable, because it stems from the fact that 'they refused to have God in

---

[1] This phrase occurs in a second-century document called the *Preaching of Peter*, quoted by Clement of Alexandria in his *Miscellanies* (vi. 5. 39); similarly another second-century work, the *Epistle to Diognetus* (ch. 1) calls Christians a 'new race' distinct from Jews and Greeks.

[2] Henry Scougall (1650-78) was appointed Professor of Divinity in King's College, Aberdeen, in 1674. His book, first published in 1677, was praised by the mother of the Wesleys as 'an excellent good book with which she had long been familiar'. Charles Wesley recommended it to George Whitefield: 'I never knew what true religion was,' he said later, 'till God sent me that excellent treatise' ... true religion being, as he learned from Scougall, 'a union of the soul with God, and Christ formed within us.' John Wesley took the book to Georgia with him, and later issued an edition of it. See G. D. Henderson, *The Burning Bush* (Edinburgh, 1957), pp. 94 ff.

their knowledge' (Rom. 1. 28). This refusal produced a spiritual
'hardening'—an insensitivity to the things of God. This word
(Gk. *pōrōsis*) appears three times in all in the New Testament;
the other two occurrences refer (i) to the synagogue audience
who would have preferred the man with the withered hand to
suffer his disability a little longer rather have it cured by Jesus
on the sabbath day (Mark 3. 5), and (ii) to the temporary spiritual
blindness under which Israel suffers until the full number of
Gentile believers is made up (Rom. 11. 25). The heart, as regularly in classical and biblical literature, is viewed as the seat of
the will and understanding, not of the emotions.

V. 19 **who being past feeling gave themselves up to
lasciviousness, to work all uncleanness with greediness.**
—To be 'past feeling' (Gk. *apalgeō*) is to have lost the sense of
pain. Just as the callous skin which grows over a severe burn
is not so sensitive as the original skin was, so in the moral life it is
possible for people to be, as Paul puts it elsewhere, 'branded in
their own conscience as with a hot iron' (1 Tim. 4. 2), incapable
of sensing the difference between right and wrong. (For
apēlgēkotes, 'having lost the sense of pain', the Western text
reads *apēlpikotes*, 'having lost hope', the perfect participle of
apelpizō; but this is less appropriate to the context.) If Paul
says here that they 'gave themselves up' to unrestrained impurity
and covetousness, he asserts with the solemn emphasis of a threefold iteration in Rom. 1. 24, 26, 28, that 'God gave them up'
to just this way of life. This way of life was theirs by choice;
they gave themselves up to it. But one of the ways in which
the wrath of God works is by giving sinners up to the course of
their own choosing, with its terrible consequences. 'Greediness'
—better 'covetousness' (Gk. *pleonexia*)—denotes not merely the
desire to possess more than one has, but more than one ought
to have, especially that which belongs by right to someone else.
In Eph. 5. 3 it is closely linked with impurity of life, and in 5. 5
it is equated with idolatry.

V. 20 **But ye did not so learn Christ;**—Christ Himself is the
embodiment of His teaching, so much so that His teaching

cannot be learned adequately without our coming to know *Him*. The apostolic preaching, by which converts were made, was the good news of what Jesus did; the apostolic teaching, by which converts were instructed in the Christian life, was based on the teaching and example of Christ. Basic to the apostolic teaching was a plain statement regarding the old vices which were to be abandoned and the new graces which were to be cultivated; this statement was frequently couched in terms of 'putting off' the old and 'putting on' the new.[1]

V. 21 **if so be that ye heard him, and were taught in him,**—If they had received even the most rudimentary fragments of Christian teaching, if they knew anything at all about Christ, they would be aware that by practice and precept He had commended a way of life vastly different from the pagan way which Paul has just described. Christ Himself is the Christians' Teacher, even if the teaching is given through the lips of His followers; to receive the teaching is in the truest sense to hear Him.

even as truth is in Jesus:—The use of the name Jesus by itself is so rare in the Pauline letters that when it occurs we look for some special significance in it, some emphasis on our Lord's historic incarnation and earthly life. In Jesus, humbling Himself in His real manhood, all truth is embodied. It was in His earthly humiliation, not in His heavenly glory, that He said: 'I am . . . the truth' (John 14. 6). Therefore to learn Him, to be 'taught in Him', is to be led into all the truth.

V. 22 **that ye put away, as concerning your former manner of life, the old man, which waxeth corrupt after the lusts of deceit;**—The old man is what they were before they became Christians, the old Adam which is our natural heritage. In Rom. 6. 6 Paul enlarges on the meaning of baptism, in which Christians are 'buried' with Christ and thus 'united with him by the likeness of his death', by affirming that 'our old

---

[1] See the exposition of Eph. 5. 21 (pp. 112 f.); cf. also E. K. Simpson and F. F. Bruce, *The Epistles of Paul to the Ephesians and to the Colossians* (Grand Rapids, 1957), pp. 264 f., with other works mentioned there in n. 37.

man was crucified with him'.   In Col. 3. 9 he reminds his readers
that they 'have put off the old man with his doings'.   But in the
present passage Christians, who (in the sense of these quotations
from other epistles) have already had their 'old man' crucified
with Christ and so have already 'put him off', are exhorted to
put him off.   The Christian ethic in the New Testament presents
a remarkable blend of the indicative and the imperative moods;
it might be summed up in the words: 'Be what you are'—'Be
in practice what you are by divine calling!'   God had called these
people out of the old life into the new, and this transition had
been symbolized in their baptism, at the very threshold of their
Christian career; but the significance of their baptism must be
spelt out in daily living.   Let that daily living proclaim as elo-
quently in one way what their baptism had proclaimed in another
way: their decisive farewell to all that they had formerly been.
This tension between the indicative and the imperative arises
from the fact that while the believer is spiritually united to Christ
at God's right hand and belongs to the age to come, yet temporally,
so long as he remains in mortal body, he lives on earth and is
involved in this present age.

As a further incentive to have done with the old man, they are
reminded that he is under sentence of death; he is undergoing
corruption by virtue of the deceitful desires which belong to his
nature.   These desires are deceitful, like the desires stirred in
our first parents by the tempter, because their gratification leads
not to a richer life, as is falsely pretended, but to eternal death.

V. 23 **and that ye be renewed in the spirit of your mind,**
—This is an echo of Rom. 12. 2, 'be ye transformed by the re-
newing of your mind'.   This inward renewal can only come
about by obedience to the apostle's next injunction:

V. 24 **and put on the new man,**—If the old man is Adam,
whose nature we inherit by birth, the new man is Christ, whose
nature is imparted to His people by their new, heavenly birth.
So, in Rom. 13. 14, when Paul commends the Christian way of
life to other readers, he sums his teaching up by saying: 'put ye
on the Lord Jesus Christ'.   Again, this is an imperative which

has its corresponding indicative: in Col. 3. 10 Christians are people who already 'have put on the new man, which is being renewed unto knowledge after the image of him that created him'. In Ephesians the adjective rendered 'new' is *kainos* (as in 2. 15)[1] whereas in the Colossians passage it is *neos*; but here at any rate it is difficult to press the usual distinction between the two words, according to which *kainos* means 'new in respect of character' while *neos* means 'new in respect of time'. Besides, while the verb 'renew' in verse 23 here is *ananeoō*, containing the element *neos*, in Col. 3. 10 it is *anakainoō*, containing *kainos*, so that each of the parallel passages brings the two words for 'new' together.

which after God hath been created in righteousness and holiness of truth.—It is not Christ personally that is 'created', of course; it is the Christ-likeness in the believer. Those who have put on the new man become like Christ, for they are God's new creation in Christ. Two essential qualities of this Christ-likeness are named—righteousness and holiness. God Himself is righteous and holy; His righteousness and holiness are perfectly manifested in Christ, and those who put on Christ are accordingly characterized by righteousness and holiness—righteousness and holiness, says Paul, which are both 'of truth',[2] of the truth as it is in Jesus. The old man and the new are alike to be recognized by the works appropriate to either.

3. Precepts of the New Life (4. 25-5. 2)

V. 25 Wherefore, putting away falsehood, speak ye truth each one with his neighbour:—The verb 'putting away' is the same as that used in verse 22 above of putting away 'the old man'; falsehood is one of his chief characteristics. Those who put off the old man and put on the new must have done with falsehood and practise truth. God is the God of truth; the

---

[1] See exposition on page 55.
[2] The construction 'righteousness and holiness of truth' may be an example of what is known as the 'Semitic genitive'; it will then mean 'true righteousness and holiness'.

devil is the father of all lying (John 8. 44). Hence the injunction comes to the children of God: 'lie not one to another' (Col. 3. 9). The positive command 'speak ye truth each one with his neighbour' is a quotation from Zech. 8. 16, where the people of Israel, restored from exile, are charged to behave in such a way as to receive God's blessing instead of incurring His wrath, as their fathers by disobedience had done.

for we are members one of another.—All deceit is an offence against God, but there is something peculiarly unnatural about deceit in the mutual relationship of those who are fellow-members of the body of Christ, who belong to one another because they belong to Him. The members cannot co-operate in harmony for the good of the whole if their dealings with one another are not marked by open-hearted sincerity and confidence.

V. 26 **Be ye angry, and sin not**:—This is a verbal reproduction of the opening words of Psa. 4. 4 in the Septuagint version; A.V. and R.V. render the Massoretic (Hebrew) text by 'Stand in awe, and sin not'. The Hebrew verb *ragaz* may denote a variety of emotional disturbances, including trembling with fear or anger. In R.S.V. the opening words of Psa. 4. 4 are rendered 'Be angry, but sin not'. What Paul means by this admonition is made plain by his following words. It is not sinful to be angry, but it is all too easy to let anger run to excess through lack of control, and righteous indignation may degenerate into sinful resentment, and can even become the first step on the road that leads to murder. Hence our Lord's solemn words about being angry with one's brother in Matt. 5. 22.[1] 'Be angry without sinning', says Paul. But how? By exercising a firm control over one's anger, and limiting its duration.

let not the sun go down upon your wrath:—'Blessed is the man who remembers this', says Polycarp in his letter to the Philippians, after he has quoted Eph. 4. 26, 'and I believe that it is so with you'. It is good to relax at the close of the day; when

---

[1] 'Every one who is angry with his brother shall be in danger of the judgement' (R.V.). It is significant that at a very early date this uncompromising statement was felt to be so intolerable that its severity was eased by the insertion of 'without a cause' after 'angry with his brother' (cf. A.V.).

tension is let go, then the Psalmist's further admonition can be
fulfilled: 'Commune with your own heart upon your bed, and
be still' (Psa. 4. 4). There can be no such heart-communing
with God in the night-watches if the sense of provocation (Gk.
parorgismos) has not first been dispelled. Even if it is not practic-
able before sundown to seek out the person who has occasioned
the anger, one can still be reconciled with him at heart by taking
the trouble to the Lord and leaving it with Him.

V. 27 **neither give place to the devil.**—Those who nurse
their wrath to keep it warm may not realize that they are giving
the devil a golden opportunity to exploit their cherished indignation to gain his own ends. But he must be allowed no room,
not the slightest foothold, within the Christian's life. The term
diabolos ('slanderer'), the Greek equivalent of the Hebrew *satan*
('adversary'), is found in the Pauline writings only in Ephesians
and in the Pastoral Epistles (cf. Eph. 6. 11);[1] Paul normally
prefers to use *satanas*, the Hebrew word supplied with a Greek
termination.

V. 28 **Let him that stole steal no more**:—This is practical
enough; the converted thief must be a thief no longer. Slaves,
for instance, had regarded petty pilfering as part of their way of
life; when they became Christians, however, they had to learn
a more excellent way. And there are more subtle breaches of
the Eighth Commandment than the picking up of unconsidered
trifles. It is no excuse for a Christian to say that 'everybody
does it'; everybody may indeed do it, but Christians have a
higher standard to maintain than the moral level of their social
groups.

**but rather let him labour, working with his hands the
thing that is good, that he may have whereof to give to
him that hath need.**—If the erstwhile thief is to give up stealing,
it follows that he must earn an honest living. But he should do
more than that, says Paul; he should work so as to earn more
than he needs for the maintenance of himself and his family, and

---

[1] In Acts 13. 10 *diabolos* appears in Paul's rebuke of Elymas the sorcerer.

7

then he will have a surplus to give to someone else—perhaps to someone who is unable, through old age or infirmity, to work for himself. Such giving is at the opposite pole from stealing; conduct like this will be a sure proof of a changed heart. Paul himself gave a fine example in this regard, when he maintained both himself and his companions by the work of his hands, rather than live at the expense of his converts (Acts 20. 34 f.; 1 Thess. 2. 9; 2 Thess. 3. 7-10).

V. 29 **Let no corrupt speech proceed out of your mouth, but such as is good for edifying as the need may be, that it may give grace to them that hear.**—In Col. 4. 6 Paul says that Christian speech should always be 'seasoned with salt'. Otherwise it may become insipid, or even worse; it may become both corrupt and corrupting. Foul language had no doubt been habitual with many of his readers before they became Christians; but such language is most unbecoming in a Christian. It must, therefore, be renounced. But the absence of such 'colourful' embellishments of talk (as they are sometimes accounted) does not mean that one's talk will become colourless. Just as the command to steal no more is followed by the positive injunction to be generous, so here the prohibition of harmful talk is accompanied by the inculcation of helpful talk. It is recorded of R. C. Chapman's home in Barnstaple: 'There was great cheerfulness at the table—words of wisdom and grace were constantly heard; but no room was given for conversation to degenerate into frivolous talk. It was also a rule of the house that no one should speak ill of an absent person, and any infringement of this rule called forth a firm though gracious reproof'.[1] Conversation with a view to timely instruction will help to build up a strong Christian character and stimulate growth in grace.

V. 30 **And grieve not the Holy Spirit of God, in whom ye were sealed unto the day of redemption.**—The Holy Spirit of God is here spoken of personally, as capable of being grieved. The implication is that unedifying language grieves the Spirit

---

[1] H. Pickering, *Chief Men Among the Brethren* (London, 1931), p. 28.

who dwells in the speaker and the hearer alike, for it tends to break down that common life in the body of Christ which it is the Spirit's province to maintain. To grieve one's brother or cause him to stumble (Rom. 14. 15, 21) is an offence against the Christian fellowship and therefore against the Spirit Himself. Paul has already reminded his readers (Eph. 1. 13 f.) that when they believed they received the seal of the Spirit, as a pledge of the inheritance which would be theirs on the day when God claimed them finally as His own possession, as a universal demonstration of His glory. That is the 'day of redemption' referred to here, the day of 'the revealing of the sons of God' (Rom. 8. 19), the day of Christ's coming 'to be glorified in his saints, and to be marvelled at in all them that believed' (2 Thess. 1. 10).

V. 31 **Let all bitterness, and wrath, and anger, and clamour, and railing, be put away from you, with all malice**:—So, lest the Spirit be grieved, let everything be put away which menaces unity of heart and purpose among believers. Annoying pinpricks and flaring outbursts of rage, public quarrelling and slanderous whispers—these and all other forms of maliciousness and ill-will must be abandoned. Such catalogues of vices are not infrequent in the New Testament writings; ugly as they are, they help to throw into clearer relief the corresponding graces, such as Paul lists in the following verse.

V. 32 **and be ye kind one to another, tenderhearted, forgiving each other, even as God also in Christ forgave you.** —Mutual kindness, compassion, and a readiness to forgive are the qualities which should characterize Christians. Most appropriately so; for they were the qualities which characterized Christ. Moreover, He ascribed these same qualities to God, and made that fact the chief reason why the children of God should exhibit them. By the exercise of love and forgiveness, He told His disciples, 'ye shall be sons of the Most High: for he is kind toward the unthankful and evil. Be ye merciful, even as your Father is merciful' (Luke 6. 35 f.). And it is the forgiving grace of God that Paul invokes here—more especially, His forgiving grace manifested in Christ—as the crowning incentive towards a spirit

of forgiveness in His children. Those who have been forgiven
so much, and at so great a cost, must be forgiving in their turn.
So, too, our Lord taught His disciples to pray, 'Forgive us our
trespasses, as we forgive them that trespass against us'—not
because our forgiving others can be the ground of God's free forgiveness of us, but because we can neither seek nor enjoy His
forgiveness so long as we cherish an unforgiving spirit to others
(Matt. 6. 12, 14 f.; 18. 21-35). Here and there in his epistles
Paul shows signs that he was acquainted with the Lord's Prayer.
The word which he uses for forgiveness in this verse is not the
common verb for remission or letting off (Gk. *aphiēmi*) but one
of richer content (Gk. *charizomai*), the word which A.V. translates
'frankly forgave' in the parable of the two debtors (Luke 7. 32);
its primary meaning is 'to grant as a free gift' and thus it is a
suitable word to denote the forgiveness of a debt.

Many ancient authorities, as R.V. margin points out, have 'us'
instead of 'you' at the end of the verse. Among these must now
be reckoned papyrus 46, which, of course,[1] was not known to the
Revisers in 1881. One reason why Greek manuscripts oscillate
so much between *hēmeis* ('we') and *hymeis* ('you') is that the
pronunciation of these two pronouns was practically identical
in the first century A.D. and onwards. Hence if a scribe was
copying by dictation, he might well put the one for the other,
especially in a context like this, where either pronoun makes
good sense.

---

[1] The Chester Beatty Biblical Papyri, of which papyrus 46 is one, did not
become known until 1931. Cf. p. 26, n. 1.

V. 1 Be ye therefore imitators of God, as beloved children;—This injunction follows on immediately from the foregoing: as God has forgiven you, says Paul, so should you forgive one another, and thus you will be imitators of God, as His dear children ought to be. Again, this echoes the Sermon on the Mount: 'Ye therefore shall be perfect, as your heavenly Father is perfect' (Matt. 5. 48, where 'perfect' may mean something like 'all-embracing in your generosity').

V. 2 and walk in love, even as Christ also loved you, and gave himself up for us, an offering and a sacrifice to God for an odour of a sweet smell.—The distribution of the pronouns 'you' and 'us' is again rather uncertain (as in 4. 32); for 'Christ also loved you', papyrus 46 (probably rightly) reads 'Christ also loved us'; and in the following clause, 'gave himself up for us', R.V. margin quotes the variant reading 'you'. The self-sacrificing love of Christ, like the Father's forgiving mercy, is an incentive and example for Christian behaviour. In His death on the cross Christ offered up His life to God as a most acceptable and all-sufficient ransom on behalf of sinners (cf. Mark 10. 45; Rom. 3. 24 f.), and His self-oblation is not infrequently described, as here, in the characteristic terminology of the Levitical law of sacrifice. The two terms for sacrifice are not technically differentiated here; where they are so differentiated, 'offering' (Gk. *prosphora*) is a meal-offering or cereal-offering (Heb. *minchah*) and 'sacrifice' (Gk. *thysia*) is a peace-offering (Heb. *zebach*).[1] The expression 'an odour of a sweet smell' occurs in a sacrificial context about forty times in the Pentateuch and four times in Ezekiel. In Phil. 4. 18 Paul uses it to describe the gift which the Philippian Christians had sent him by the hand of Epaphroditus. It is pre-eminently by the

---

[1] The two terms are used of our Lord's oblation several times in Hebrews: *prosphora* in Heb. 10. 10, 14, and *thysia* in Heb. 9. 26; 10. 26. In Rom. 8. 3 and 2 Cor. 5. 21 Paul describes His death as a sin-offering (Heb. *hatta'th* or *'asham*, the latter word being used of the Servant's self-offering in Isa. 53. 10).

imitation of God in Christ that the change from the old way of
life to the new is to be manifested; the life in which this change
has taken place becomes in its turn a fragrant offering to God,
'a sweet savour of Christ' (2 Cor. 2. 15).

4. OLD DARKNESS AND NEW LIGHT (5. 3-21)

V. 3 **But fornication, and all uncleanness, or covetousness, let it not even be named among you, as becometh
saints**;—Catalogues of vices were common form in the writings
of pagan moralists and in Jewish polemic against paganism; they
are found frequently in Paul's epistles (cf. Rom. 1. 29 ff.; 1 Cor.
5. 11; 6. 9 f.; Gal. 5. 19 ff.; Col. 3. 5 ff.), but in Paul's epistles
they derive a special significance from the Christian context in
which he sets them.   Fornication and other forms of unclean
living were certainly sins against which converts from paganism
needed to be put on their guard, as is particularly evident from
Paul's Corinthian correspondence.   We may think it strange to
see covetousness so closely associated with these vices, but Paul
is simply moving from outward manifestations of sin to their inner
springs in the cravings of the heart.   We may remember how
our Lord similarly traces murder back to the angry thought, and
adultery to the lustful glance (Matt. 5. 21 ff., 27 ff.).   Covetousness (Gk. *pleonexia*) has already been mentioned (Eph. 4. 19) as
a feature of pagan behaviour.   Occasionally it has special reference
to trespassing in the sexual sphere, as in 1 Thess. 4. 6, where
Paul enjoins that no one should 'wrong his brother'—literally,
'act covetously (Gk. *pleonektein*) against him'—by seeking illicit
relations with one of the women in his family circle.   But covetousness may assume a much more respectable form than this,
and is all the more dangerous on that account.   Together with
the other sins mentioned, far from being practised in the Christian
circle, it should not even be mentioned in it.   For Christians are
the holy people of God, and such unholy things are unfitting for
their minds to dwell upon or their tongues to name.

V. 4 **nor filthiness, nor foolish talking, or jesting, which
are not befitting**:—From the company which it keeps here,

'filthiness' (Gk. *aischrotēs*) is probably to be understood in the same sense as the 'shameful speaking' (Gk. *aischrologia*) of Col. 3. 8. Ribaldry, buffoonery and flippancy are wholly incongruous on Christian lips. 'A merry heart is a good medicine' (Prov. 17. 22), and Paul commends the speech that is 'seasoned with salt' (Col. 4. 6); but coarse vulgarity is to be avoided, and still more so that 'jesting' (Gk. *eutrapelia*) which Aristotle[1] defines as 'cultured insolence'. Above all, light and irreverent talk about sacred things is to be utterly reprobated.

but rather giving of thanks.—'Our tongues were made to bless the Lord', as Isaac Watts reminds us, and Christian tongues in particular have unbounded cause for engaging in this most worthy activity. Tongues which are habituated to the praise of God should not readily lend themselves to language which dishonours His name.

V. 5 For this ye know of a surety, that no fornicator, nor unclean person, nor covetous man, which is an idolater, hath any inheritance in the kingdom of Christ and God.— A solemn warning accompanies the apostle's ban on impurity in deed, thought or word. The opening words of the verse may be taken either as indicative (so R.V., as quoted above), or as imperative: 'Be well assured of this' (Gk. *iste ginōskontes*, literally 'know ye knowing'). No one who is guilty of the vicious practices mentioned has any share in the heavenly kingdom. Only the regenerate can enter the kingdom of God, and these practices bear witness to an unregenerate heart, whatever professions may be made to the contrary. The idea that Paul means that such people may be true Christians even so, but that their behaviour will debar them from any part or lot in a future millennial reign of Christ, is totally unwarranted by the context and by New Testament teaching in general. In the similar passage in 1 Cor. 6. 9-11, it is abundantly clear that 'the unrighteous' who, because of various specified vices, 'shall not inherit the kingdom of God' are distinct from those who have been 'washed, . . . sanctified, . . .

[1] *Rhetoric* ii. 12.

justified in the name of the Lord Jesus Christ, and in the Spirit of our God'. A covetous man, says Paul, is an idolater (cf. Col. 3. 5), because he sets his affections on earthly things and not on things above, and so puts some other object of desire in the central place which God alone should have in the human heart.[1] The part which the commandment against covetousness played in Paul's own spiritual experience (Rom. 7. 7 ff.) no doubt made him acutely aware of the special deadliness of this subtle sin. The expression 'the kingdom of Christ and God' does not denote two separate kingdoms, but one, the kingdom which is Christ's and God's. Paul perhaps uses the term 'kingdom of Christ' for the present phase of the divine kingdom, when it is mediatorially administered by Christ, reserving the term 'kingdom of God' for its future consummation in full glory. (Sometimes, however, he speaks of the 'kingdom of God' with a more general reference.) The wording in our present passage implies that both phases are conjoined; neither here nor hereafter can there be any place for impenitent sinners in that kingdom which is 'righteousness and peace and joy in the Holy Spirit' (Rom. 14. 17).

V. 6 **Let no man deceive you with empty words: for because of these things cometh the wrath of God upon the sons of disobedience.**—Some forms of Gnosticism in the second century and onwards, of which adumbrations can be traced even in the first century, held that such practices as the apostle here condemns were irrelevant to the spiritual life, because they had to do with the body, whereas the spiritual life was concerned only with the soul. In addition, it is plain from some of Paul's other letters that his converts in certain places were apt to be misled by the argument that freedom from the law implied freedom to sin—to sin in order that God's grace might abound the more (cf. Rom. 6. 1). Paul characterizes all such sophistries as 'empty words'—we may compare the 'vain deceit' against which he warns the Colossians in Col. 2. 8. His readers must be on their guard against such specious talk, lest they be seduced

---

[1] Cf. Eph. 4. 19 and 5. 3, with accompanying exposition (pp. 92, 102).

by it. It is precisely this sort of behaviour, he says, that brings down the wrath of God on the 'sons of disobedience' (a description of the ungodly repeated from Eph. 2. 2). This is a theme which he elaborates especially in Rom. 1. 18 ff., where he shows the successive stages in which 'the wrath of God is revealed from heaven against all ungodliness and unrighteousness of men'. God has written His decree against such sins in the very constitution and conscience of men; how then can those who are peculiarly His people tolerate them in their personal and social life?

V. 7 **Be not ye therefore partakers with them**;—The Greek word rendered 'partaker' (*symmetochos*) is one of Paul's characteristic compounds with the prefix *syn*. In Eph. 3. 6, as we have seen, he uses it of Gentile believers who are joint-sharers with Jewish believers in the body of Christ; here, contrariwise, it is used of partnership in iniquity.

V. 8 **for ye were once darkness, but are now light in the Lord**:—The opposed themes of light and darkness are frequently used in the New Testament to denote the divine kingdom as against all that is contrary to it, especially in the Johannine and Pauline writings. The basic principle of this opposition is stated most succinctly in 1 John 1. 5, 'God is light, and in him is no darkness at all'. The calling forth of light from darkness in the creation narrative of Gen. 1. 2 ff. is used as a picture of the expulsion of moral darkness by the inflowing of heavenly light (2 Cor. 4. 6). The Eternal Word, agent of God in the first creation, is the very embodiment of heavenly light and shines in His incarnation as 'the light of the world' (John 8. 12; 9. 5), 'the light which lighteth every man' (John 1. 9). Evildoers hate and shun the light; 'he that doeth the truth cometh to the light' (John 3. 20 f.). In Col. 1. 13 Christians are said to have been rescued from the dominion of darkness and brought over into the realm where Christ reigns as king, the inheritance of light which is reserved for the people of God. So here, the Christians addressed are described as having formerly been not merely *in* darkness, but darkness itself, during their years of paganism; through faith-union with Christ, however, they have become light in Him.

walk as children of light—'Children of light' (Gk. *tekna phōtos*), like the synonymous 'sons of light' (*hyioi phōtos*) in Luke 16. 8 and 1 Thess. 5. 5, is an expression denoting those whose lives are characterized by divine light, since they are begotten of God and do His will. The expression has gained further currency in recent years from its use in Qumran literature (especially in the *Rule of War*, frequently entitled *The War of the Sons of Light with the Sons of Darkness*[1]), but this need not indicate a *direct* relationship between the Qumran texts and the New Testament, since both bodies of literature shared a common background. To 'walk as children of light' means to behave as Christians ought (cf. 1 Thess. 5. 8; 1 John 1. 6 f.).

V. 9 **(for the fruit of the light is in all goodness and righteousness and truth),**—The 'Received Text' reads 'the fruit of the Spirit' (so A.V.), under the influence of Gal. 5. 22; but, although it has the unusually strong support of papyrus 46, it must be regarded as inferior to the reading 'the fruit of the light'. This latter reading is confirmed not only by the weight of the evidence, but also by the context, in view both of the general theme of light in these verses and of the counterbalancing reference to 'the unfruitful works of darkness' in verse 11. The fruit of the light is simply the manner of life produced in believers by the true light which dwells within them—a manner of life marked by 'goodness and righteousness and truth'.

V. 10 **proving what is well-pleasing unto the Lord;**— The verb translated 'proving' is *dokimazō*, which may mean not only putting to the test but approving as good. We may 'prove' what is well-pleasing to the Lord by putting it into practice, but we may also, by our practical experience of it, learn to *approve* the will of God, as being 'good and acceptable and perfect' (Rom. 12. 2, where the same verb is used). This fuller meaning of the word is probably intended here.

---

[1] Similarly in the Qumran *Rule of the Community* (frequently entitled the *Manual of Discipline*) all mankind are divided by divine predestination into two categories, the 'sons of light' under the rule of the 'prince of lights' and the 'sons of deceit' under the rule of the 'angel of darkness'. (Cf. p. 32, n. 1; p. 65, n. 1.)

V. 11 **and have no fellowship with the unfruitful works of darkness,**—In Gal. 5. 19-23 the 'works of the flesh' are contrasted with the 'fruit of the Spirit', perhaps with the implication that the 'flesh'—the old nature—is a dead thing whose manifestations cannot properly be described as 'fruit'. If that is so, it is evidently the same idea that finds expression here; the works of darkness, the practices which characterized paganism, are 'unfruitful' and sterile, issuing in death.

but rather even reprove them;—If the things which please God are to be approved, the things which displease Him are naturally to be reprobated—exposed, censured and, if possible, corrected (Gk. *elenchō*).

V. 12 **for the things which are done by them in secret it is a shame even to speak of.**—The very mention of such vices is offensive to people who are morally sensitive, although their exposure, in accordance with the apostle's injunction, may require such outspokenness as he himself uses, for example, in Rom. 1. 24-32.

V. 13 **But all things when they are reproved are made manifest by the light: for everything that is made manifest is light.**—When these things are exposed (the verb *elenchō* is used again) by being dragged out of the dingy corners where they lurk into the light of day, they are seen for what they are, in all their ugliness. But evidently along with the idea of exposure goes that of correction; when they are brought into the light such evils must wither and die. The light is, of course, the light of God. The statement that 'everything that is made manifest (Gk. *phaneroō*) is light' implies that when a man abandons the darkness of sin and comes to the light, he enters that company of which Paul has just said: 'ye were once darkness, but are now light in the Lord' (v. 8). The teaching is very similar to that of John 3. 20 f.: 'every one that doeth ill hateth the light, and cometh not to the light, lest his works should be reproved (Gk. *elenchō*); but he that doeth the truth cometh to the light, that his works may be made manifest (Gk. *phaneroō*), that they have been wrought in God'.

V. 14 Wherefore *he* saith, Awake, thou that sleepest, and arise from the dead, and Christ shall shine upon thee.— The introductory formula (Gk. *dio legei*) is used in Eph. 4. 8 to introduce a biblical quotation. In the present instance, while the words which follow represent the general sense of a number of Old Testament passages (cf. Isa. 26. 19; 51. 17; 52. 1; 60. 1; Mal. 4. 2), they are not as they stand derived from any single Old Testament context. In Greek they form a metrical triplet, the rhythm of which can easily be reproduced in English, thus:

> Awake, O thou that sleepest,
> And from the dead arouse thee,
> And Christ shall dawn upon thee.

It is significant that in the Hellenistic world this precise rhythm was specially associated with religious initiation-chants,[1] and it has been suggested that Christians took the rhythm over for use in the act of Christian initiation, and that we have here a primitive baptismal hymn. Baptism symbolizes the convert's emergence from the darkness of the tomb to the light of resurrection-life, and one of the names by which it came to be called in the Early Church was 'enlightenment' (Gk. *phōtismos*), a designation possibly used as early as Heb. 6. 4; 10. 32. This interpretation of Eph. 5. 14 cannot be demonstrated to be the true one, but it is more probable than any other. In that case, the impersonal 'wherefore it saith' (cf. R.S.V., 'Therefore it is said') would be a preferable rendering to 'wherefore he saith' of A.V. and R.V.

The verb 'shine' (Gk. *epiphauskō*) is used of the rising of a heavenly body. In some texts the future *epiphausei* ('shall shine upon') has been corrupted to *epipsausei* ('shall touch'), and in others the resultant 'Christ shall touch thee' has been further changed so as to read 'thou shalt touch Christ'; but such readings are poorly supported and in any case are alien intruders upon the figure of illumination.

V. 15 Look therefore carefully how ye walk,—This order,

---

[1] Such as the Attis formula quoted by Firmicus Maternus (*Error of Profane Religions*, 18) and the Eleusinian formula quoted by Clement of Alexandria (*Exhortation to the Heathen*, 2. 14).

in which 'carefully' (Gk. *akribōs*) precedes 'how' (Gk. *pōs*), is slightly better attested than that which in 'how' precedes 'carefully' (whence A.V. 'see then that ye walk circumspectly', where the adverb modifies 'walk' instead of 'look'). 'Pay careful heed to your behaviour', says the apostle, resuming the injunction at the end of verse 8.

not as unwise, but as wise;—We may compare Col. 4. 5, 'walk in wisdom toward them that are without'. Especially in view of the slanderous reports which circulated about Christian behaviour, it was important that Christians should so conduct themselves that everyone might see how false these reports were. More generally, the apostle echoes his Master's direction to His disciples to be 'wise as serpents, and harmless as doves' (Matt. 10. 16), as he also does in Rom. 16. 19 when he urges his readers to be 'wise unto that which is good, and simple unto that which is evil'. (The same Greek adjective, *akeraios*, is rendered 'harmless' in Matt. 10. 16 and 'simple' in Rom. 16. 19.)

V. 16 **redeeming the time, because the days are evil.** —The Colossian Christians are urged to redeem the time with a special view to their witness among unbelieving neighbours (Col. 4. 5); here the injunction has more general regard to the duty of Christian prudence. The days were 'evil'; persecution and distress threatened the churches throughout the Roman Empire; signs were not lacking of the impending fall of the Second Jewish Commonwealth, with all the incalculable implications which that might have for the Christian cause. The present opportunity for Christian life and work might not last much longer; Christians should therefore use it to the full while they could. The word translated 'time' (Gk. *kairos*) denotes a critical epoch, a special opportunity, which may soon pass; 'grasp it', says the apostle, 'buy it up for yourselves (Gk. *exagorazomai*) while it lasts'.

V. 17 **Wherefore be ye not foolish, but understand what the will of the Lord is.**—Failure to appraise and utilize the passing opportunity would be disastrous folly. It is so in ordinary commercial and political affairs; it is not less so in the spiritual realm. The opportunities which come our way in Christian experience are opportunities for doing the will of God, but in order to do it we must understand what it is, and such understanding can only come by paying heed to His Word and applying it to the requirements of the day through the wisdom which His Spirit bestows. In fact, to 'understand what the will of the Lord is' is little different from 'proving what is well-pleasing unto the Lord'—the phrase which has been used above in verse 10.

V. 18 **And be not drunken with wine, wherein is riot,** —The first clause is a quotation from the Septuagint of Prov. 23. 30. Over-indulgence in wine was a common enough vice in the world of the New Testament, to judge from the repeated warnings against it scattered throughout the apostolic writings. Drunkenness is one of 'the works of the flesh' listed in Gal. 5. 19-21, and excludes one from inheritance in the kingdom of God (cf. 1 Cor. 6. 10). It leads to other forms of profligacy— the 'riotous living' of the prodigal son (Luke 15. 13)—and in particular it makes it impossible to exercise the prudent recognition and exploitation of fleeting opportunity which the present context enjoins.

but be filled with the Spirit;—The effects of being filled with the Spirit were mockingly misinterpreted on the day of Pentecost as being the result of new wine (Acts 2. 13); but neither there nor here is it to be inferred that the Spirit is a substance with which man's personality can be filled just as his body can be filled with wine. Paul does not say, 'Become full of the Spirit' but (literally), 'Be filled in Spirit'; and if we wish to know what he means by the phrase 'in Spirit', we may consider its occurrence in three other places in this epistle (Eph. 2. 22; 3. 5; 6. 18), where the personal operation of the Holy Spirit is in view. Instead of seeking such satisfaction as some expect to find through wine-bibbing, he means, let your fulness be that which the Holy Spirit produces. Some of the symptoms of this spiritual fulness are mentioned in the following verses.

V. 19 **speaking one to another in psalms and hymns and spiritual songs, singing and making melody with your**

heart to the Lord;—Praise such as is described here both
glorifies God and edifies man. 'Speaking one to another' corresponds to the fuller phrase 'teaching and admonishing one
another' in Col. 3. 16. If we are to distinguish between the three
kinds of musical composition,[1] 'psalms' may refer to the Old
Testament Psalter, which has provided a perennial source of
Christian praise from the earliest times; 'hymns' may denote
Christian canticles such as have been recognized in several
places in the New Testament (including verse 14 above);[2] 'spiritual
songs' may be unpremeditated words sung 'in the Spirit', voicing
praise and holy aspirations. We have evidence from various
writers of the way in which early Christians 'spoke one to another'
in sacred song.[3] Pliny, when Roman governor of Bithynia in
A.D. 112, was told how the Christians of his province were in the
habit of meeting on a fixed day before dawn and 'reciting a hymn
antiphonally to Christ as God'.[4] Towards the end of the same
century Tertullian, writing in North Africa, describes the Christian love-feast at which 'each is invited to sing to God in the
presence of the others from what he knows of the holy scripture
or from his own heart'.[5] The verb translated 'making melody'
(Gk. *psallō*) means originally plucking the strings of a lyre or
similar instrument, but this etymological sense is probably not
intended here; we may take it in the sense of singing psalms
which it has in 1 Cor. 14. 15 and Jas. 5. 13. (It is, in fact, the
word from which 'psalm' is derived.) The context in which it
occurs in 1 Cor. 14. 15, 'I will sing with the spirit, and I will
sing with the understanding also', chimes in well with the apostle's
insistence here, that such melody, to be acceptable to the Lord,
must spring from the heart. We may also compare Col. 3. 16,

---

[1] It is unlikely that the reference is restricted to three types of composition
represented within the Old Testament Psalter, designated respectively by the
Hebrew names *mizmor*, *tehillah* and *shir*.

[2] Several of the lyric passages in the book of Revelation were probably sung
in Christian worship as hymns of praise.

[3] We may think of the early Christian hymn book curiously called the *Odes
of Solomon*; or the *Song of the Star* in Ignatius's letter to the Ephesians (19. 2 f.).

[4] *Epistle to Trajan* (x. 96.)

[5] *Apology*, 39.

'singing with grace in your hearts unto God', where 'grace' (Gk. *charis*) means thanksgiving. Nothing yields worthy praise more spontaneously than a thankful heart. So the apostle continues:

V. 20 **giving thanks always for all things in the name of our Lord Jesus Christ to God, even the Father**;—This might seem a counsel of perfection, did we not know full well that Paul himself had learned to do this very thing, even in the most un-propitious circumstances. The man who, with his companion, sang hymns to God at midnight in the cramping discomfort of the Philippian stocks has a right to recommend the same attitude of heart to others. Thanksgiving is properly rendered to God in the name of Christ, not only because He is the One through whom we approach God, but also because He Himself constitutes our crowning subject for thanksgiving. It is when we appreciate the grace of God in not sparing His own Son, but giving Him up for us all, that we can best appreciate God's further grace in freely giving us all things with Him (Rom. 8. 32). And it is when we learn by experience that, to those who love Him, God makes all things work together for good (Rom. 8. 28), that we can wholeheartedly give Him thanks 'always for all things'. Those who have learned this lesson will be able not only to give thanks to God through Christ but to fulfil the even more com-prehensive injunction of the parallel passage in Col. 3. 17: 'And whatsoever ye do, in word or in deed, do all in the name of the Lord Jesus, giving thanks to God the Father through him.'

V. 21 **subjecting yourselves one to another in the fear of Christ.**—The present section of the epistle comes to an end with a general exhortation to mutual deference and service, which finds particular application in the following verses to the various relations within the Christian household. From the ethical sections of the New Testament epistles it has been inferred that in the earliest days of Christianity a fairly uniform body of teach-ing about Christian behaviour was communicated to the infant churches.[1] The steady increase in the number of Gentile con-

---

[1] Cf. Eph. 4. 20 with accompanying exposition (p. 93).

verts made it desirable that they should learn the rudiments of Christian ethics in a readily assimilated form. The teaching which was imparted to them was in essence the teaching of Christ Himself, classified in groups of injunctions each of which was introduced by a sort of catchword. We have already met the catchwords 'put off' and 'put on' (Eph. 4. 22, 24); 'subjecting yourselves' is another. It is easier to pay lip-service to the duty of mutual submission than to practise it, but when it is undertaken in a spirit of reverence for Christ it can be achieved. When Peter enjoins this same attitude, he does so in words which recall Christ's own example in girding Himself with a towel to perform a lowly service for His disciples: 'Yea, all of you gird yourselves with humility, to serve one another' (1 Pet. 5. 5; cf. John 13. 4 f.).

5. THE CHRISTIAN HOUSEHOLD (5. 22-6. 9)

The graces which ought to flourish in the Christian fellowship might be expected to find a specially congenial environment in the Christian household. Here pre-eminently should mutual consideration and deference be shown, between husbands and wives, between parents and children, between masters and servants. Codes of domestic behaviour were common form among the Gentile moralists of the day, and it is interesting to compare them with the instruction given about family life in the New Testament. From the way in which this kind of instruction recurs in various New Testament writings (cf. Col. 3. 18-4. 1; 1 Tim. 3. 4 f., 12; 5. 14; 6. 1 f.; Titus 2. 1-10; 1 Pet. 2. 13-3. 7), it has been inferred that it regularly formed part of a fairly well defined body of practical teaching imparted to Christian converts. Many of the mutual family duties inculcated in these New Testament passages can be paralleled in contemporary non-Christian literature, but the New Testament raises the whole situation on to a higher level by relating each of these duties to the Christian faith. Obedience and submission on the one part, like love and care on the other part, are enjoined for Christ's sake.

8

5a *Wives and Husbands* (5. 22-33)

V. 22 **Wives,** *be in subjection* **unto your own husbands, as unto the Lord.**—In verse 22 the words 'be in subjection' are italicized in the text because they are absent from the Greek; they have to be supplied from verse 21, 'subjecting yourselves one to another in the fear of Christ'. The deference which wives are to show to their husbands is a particular aspect of that submission which all Christians have been urged to show to one another. Other moralists insisted that the subordination of wives to their husbands was right because it was part of the natural order of things; Paul inculcates it as a Christian duty. The phrase 'as unto the Lord' does not mean that they should yield to their husbands the same deference as they would yield to Christ Himself, but that deference to their husbands is a duty which they owe to the Lord. It is not that women are inferior to men, or that wives are inferior to their husbands, either naturally or spiritually. But Paul recognizes a divinely ordained hierarchy in the order of creation, and in this order the wife has a place next after her husband. When she recognizes and accepts this subordinate place, he means, she does so 'as unto the Lord', acknowledging His ordinance.

V. 23 **For the husband is the head of the wife, as Christ also is the head of the church,** *being* **himself the saviour of the body.**—Paul had already stated in 1 Cor. 11. 3 that 'the head of every man is Christ; and the head of the woman is the man; and the head of Christ is God'. Thus he establishes the hierarchy ascending from woman through man through Christ to God. Here he recasts this conception in the light of the teaching given already in this epistle about Christ as the head of the Church. If the head of the woman is the man, and the head of the Church is Christ, then an analogy can be drawn between a wife's relation to her husband and the Church's relation to Christ. The Church owes obedience to Christ; so, too, does a wife to her husband. As Christ is the deliverer and defender of the Church which is His body, so (the implication seems to be) the husband is the protector of his wife, who (according to the Genesis narrative) is 'one flesh' with him.

V. 24 **But as the church is subject to Christ, so** *let* **the wives also** *be* **to their husbands in everything.**—Paul might have gone on to develop the significance of Christ's being 'the saviour of the body', but he comes back to the subject with which he is dealing—the wife's duty of submission or deference. Here the verb 'be in subjection' is expressed, and not left to be understood as in verse 22. The wife's special deference to her husband takes its character from the special relationship which binds husband and wife together—a relationship which Paul illuminates by presenting it as analogous to that supernatural relationship in which the Church is bound to Christ. But if he places the duties of wives on such a lofty plane, he rates the obligations of husbands no lower.

V. 25 **Husbands, love your wives, even as Christ also loved the church, and gave himself up for it**;—The wife's submission to her husband has as its correlative his duty to love her—with a love which is much more than natural affection or attraction, involving his active and unceasing and self-sacrificing concern for her well-being. The Church's obedience to Christ, which is the wife's model for her duty to her husband, may fall short of what it should be; there are no shortcomings about the love of Christ for His Church, which is here prescribed as the model for the Christian husband's love for his wife. By setting this highest of standards for the husband's treatment of his wife, Paul goes to the limit in safeguarding the wife's dignity and welfare. For the love of Christ is a self-giving love: He gave Himself up for His Church, and the natural inference is that there is no sacrifice, not even the sacrifice of his life, which a husband should not be prepared to make, if necessary, for his wife.

V. 26 **that he might sanctify it, having cleansed it by the washing of water with the word,**—Having stated that Christ gave Himself up for the sake of His Church, the apostle goes on to elaborate the purpose of this self-sacrifice, in language which for the time being leaves the husband-wife relationship far behind, and indeed out of sight. Christ's intention was to have the Church as His own possession, the community of His holy people, set apart for Himself. But to this end the Church must be cleansed; the defilement which had previously adhered to its members must be washed away. This cleansing He Himself has effected, by means of the 'washing with water, accompanied by a spoken word' (for so we may paraphrase the expression here used). This washing with water, accompanied by a spoken word, can scarcely be anything other than baptism; this is what the language would most naturally have conveyed to the original readers. Many Protestant commentators have strenuously resisted this exegesis, mainly because it seems to lend itself too easily to a perverted doctrine of 'baptismal regeneration'—that is the idea that the external application of water, accompanied by the appropriate words, is sufficient to bring about regeneration. To this perversion, needless to say, the New Testament gives no countenance; regeneration is an inward change wrought by the Holy Spirit, and the cleansing of which Paul speaks is likewise an inward experience; but the regeneration and the cleansing alike are symbolized and signified in baptism.[1] The 'washing of water' is the same washing as is called the 'washing of regeneration' in Titus 3. 5. (The alternative rendering 'laver', proposed by R.V. margin in both places, is not to be preferred.) The 'word' which accompanies the washing is an utterance, a spoken word (Gk. *rhēma*)—either the word which is spoken *over* the person being baptized, pronouncing the Holy Name upon him (cf. Matt. 28. 19; Acts 2. 38; 8. 16, etc.), or (more probably) the word spoken *by* him, in which he confesses his faith and invokes the Lord. So Paul himself was commanded by Ananias: 'arise, and be baptized, and wash away thy sins, *calling on his name*'

---

[1] Cf. Eph. 4. 5 with accompanying exposition (pp. 78 ff.). 'If "having cleansed it with the washing of water with the word" is intended to signify what happened at baptism, then the idea is consistent with the association of purification with the symbolism of baptism. Each individual member of the Church had become dedicated to God at the time of his symbolic purification from sin; and what happened to each separate individual is said to have happened to the entire New Society' (A. Borland in *The Believer's Magazine*, September 1954, p. 174).

(Acts 22. 16). In our present passage the noun *rhēma* is preceded by the preposition *en* ('in'), which should, perhaps, be regarded here as having 'comitative' force; hence the suggested rendering, 'accompanied by a spoken word'.

V. 27 **that he might present the church to himself a glorious** *church*, **not having spot or wrinkle or any such thing; but that it should be holy and without blemish.**—The Church, viewed here in the light of her Lord's purpose, is the Church in perfected glory. The Church as it is seen in our actual experience at the present time falls far short of this ideal; spots and wrinkles are abundantly in evidence. C. S. Lewis's demon, Screwtape, draws a contrast between the Church as she is seen 'spread out through all time and space and rooted in eternity, terrible as an army with banners', and the Church as people meet it in ordinary life; and suggests that the anticlimax of the contrast can be used to weaken a new convert's faith and zeal.[1] But the contrast can work in the opposite way and help us to glorify the grace of God; when we look at the church members we know—better still, when we look at ourselves as we are—and then consider what Christ has already done with such unpromising material, and what He is yet going to make of it, the wonder of His redeeming purpose may well call forth our worship and stimulate us to live lives more worthy of the calling with which He has called us. The day on which He will present the glorified Church to Himself is, of course, the day of His own advent in glory, when His people are to be glorified with Him. This, as Paul has told us at the beginning of the epistle, was what God had in view when He chose His people in Christ before the world's foundation (Eph. 1. 14).

V. 28 **Even so ought husbands also to love their own wives as their own bodies.**—Paul now reverts to the married relationship. To Christian readers in the western world today he may appear to be rubbing in the husband's duty of love to his wife with unnecessary and repetitive emphasis; we may be dis-

---

[1] *The Screwtape Letters* (London, 1942), pp. 15 f.

posed to think that this is one of the lessons which nature itself teaches us. But that is not so; some acquaintance with the pagan world of New Testament times, or with many areas of human life today, will show us how necessary this insistence was, and still is; and it may suggest that if we are inclined to take this lesson for granted, that is the measure of the effectiveness of the apostle's teaching on the subject in those places where the gospel has been most influential. Paul does not overdo the analogy and speak of the wife as her husband's body, as the Church is Christ's body; but the Old Testament teaching that husband and wife are 'one flesh', which he quotes below, is sufficient justification for his ruling that a husband should love his wife as his own body.

He that loveth his own wife loveth himself:—Properly speaking there is no altruism in a man's love of his wife (or family); from the biblical point of view his wife (like his family) is an extension of his own personality. To treat one's wife as a slave or a chattel does as much damage to a man's own personality as to hers.

V. 29 for no man ever hated his own flesh; but nourisheth and cherisheth it,—Asceticism for asceticism's sake—that 'severity to the body' which is mentioned with disapproval in Col. 2. 23—is unnatural, and plays no part in New Testament Christianity. The self-discipline described by Paul in 1 Cor. 9. 27 and elsewhere comes into quite a different category. The second great commandment, 'Thou shalt love thy neighbour as thyself' (Lev. 19. 18), implies that self-injury is as improper as it is unnatural. And if one's neighbour is to be so loved (in the meaning given to the commandment by our Lord in the parable of the good Samaritan), how much more one's wife! The care which a man bestows upon his body as a matter of course, in feeding and clothing it and generally looking after its health and comfort, should equally be bestowed upon his wife.

even as Christ also the church;—Everything that the Church requires for her sustenance and well-being she receives as a gift from her exalted Lord (cf. Eph. 4. 7 ff.).

V. 30 because we are members of his body.—As those

who are one with Him, part of Him, incorporated into Him, the people of Christ are the objects of His special care. The A.V., following the 'Received Text' and the later manuscripts and versions, adds: 'of his flesh, and of his bones'—an echo of Gen. 2. 23, where Adam greets Eve as 'bone of my bones, and flesh of my flesh'. The addition, while not original, is quite in keeping with the argument of the passage, especially as the apostle goes on immediately to quote Gen. 2. 24.

V. 31 **For this cause shall a man leave his father and mother, and shall cleave to his wife; and the twain shall become one flesh.**—Our Lord quotes these words in Mark 10. 7 f. to show that marriage is a lifelong union; Paul quotes them here to show the vital unity into which the marriage bond brings husband and wife. The Massoretic text of the Hebrew simply says 'they shall be one flesh'; the expression 'the twain' comes from the Septuagint, but it may very well have been found in a variant and earlier form of the Hebrew text.[1]

V. 32 **This mystery is great: but I speak in regard of Christ and of the church.**—That is to say, the words of Gen. 2. 24 enshrine a greater truth than that which lies on the surface— a truth which Paul indicates without developing it in the present passage. 'But I for my part', he adds—referring to the special revelation committed to him concerning the Church as the body of Christ—'am applying it to Christ and to the Church'. In other words, 'I am treating the man as symbolic of Christ and the woman as symbolic of the Church'.

V. 33 **Nevertheless do ye also severally love each one his own wife even as himself;**—For the present, however, the practical lesson is what matters: each husband must treat his wife no worse than he would treat himself; her welfare is indissolubly bound up with his own.

and *let* **the wife** *see* **that she fear her husband.**—'Fear', of course, in the sense of reverence or respect; the R.V. here has

---

[1] It is attested not only by the Septuagint but also by the Samaritan Bible, by the Palestinian and Samaritan Targums, by the Syriac Peshitta and by the Latin Vulgate.

not made an improvement by departing from the A.V. wording: 'and the wife see that she reverence her husband'. (It need hardly be said that if the wife is to reverence her husband, he has an obligation to deserve her reverence.) Similarly in 1 Pet. 3. 1-6 Christian wives are urged to show the same deference to their husbands as was shown by the 'holy women' of Old Testament days, like Sarah, whose daughters they would prove themselves to be if they persisted in welldoing and were not 'put in fear by any terror'. The Greek verb rendered 'put in fear' in 1 Pet. 3. 6 is the same (*phobeomai*) as is rendered 'fear' (R.V.) or 'reverence' (A.V.) in Eph. 5. 33; but is clearly used in two widely differing senses in the two places.

CHAPTER VI

5b. *Children and Parents* (6. 1-4)

V. 1 **Children, obey your parents in the Lord: for this is right.**—From the mutual duties of husbands and wives, Paul passes to those of children and parents. He has a Christian family in view ('in the Lord'), and does not contemplate the situation where parental orders might be contrary to the law of Christ. In the last resort, the law of Christ must take precedence. Disobedience to parents is a symptom of the disintegration of society (cf. Rom. 1. 30; 2 Tim. 3. 3); Christian families should, by the example they show, put a check upon disintegrating tendencies in their environment. 'This is right' (Gk. *dikaios*), says the apostle here; 'this is well-pleasing in the Lord', he says in the parallel passage in Col. 3. 20. And it has already been enjoined in the Old Testament law.

V. 2 **Honour thy father and mother (which is the first commandment with promise),**—The fifth commandment (Exod. 20. 12; Deut. 5. 16) is not only the first commandment in the decalogue with a promise annexed (the words about God's mercy to those who love Him and keep His commandments at the end of the second commandment are a declaration of God's character rather than a promise); it is the only such commandment in the decalogue. But when Paul calls it 'the first commandment with promise' he is thinking not only of the decalogue but of the whole body of Pentateuchal legislation which is introduced by the decalogue.

V. 3 **that it may be well with thee, and thou mayest live long on the earth.**—This is the Deuteronomic form of the commandment in the Septuagint version. Long life in the land of Israel is a reward held out for the keeping of the divine law in general, and not only for this commandment in particular (cf. Deut. 4. 40; 5. 33). Paul, of course, omits the specific reference to the land of Israel, as being inapplicable in this wider setting.

V. 4 **And, ye fathers, provoke not your children to wrath:**

but nurture them in the chastening and admonition of the Lord.—Parents (for the plural *pateres* may mean this rather than simply 'fathers') have an obligation to their children as well as children to their parents; if children must obey their parents, parents should deserve their children's obedience. It is possible, even for Christian parents, to be so unreasonable in their demands on their children that the children are irritated beyond measure and wonder whether it does any good to try to please their parents and do what they say. Children should be brought up 'in the discipline (*paideia*) and instruction (*nouthesia*) of the Lord' (R.S.V.); since they are a 'heritage of the Lord' (Psa. 127. 3), their training should be undertaken with a sense of responsibility to Him, so that from their early days they may learn to worship and love Him.

5c. Servants and Masters (6. 5-9)

V. 5 Servants, be obedient unto them that according to the flesh are your masters,—In Ephesians, as in Colossians and 1 Peter, the injunctions to slaves are more extended than those to masters, and are accompanied by special encouragements. This may well reflect the social structure of the churches addressed. The Epistle to Philemon provides an illuminating commentary on the mutual duties of slaves and masters within the Christian fellowship, and the transforming influence of this fellowship on their relations with one another. The slave-master relationship belongs to the passing temporal order; it is a relationship 'according to the flesh'. In the spiritual realm, Christian slaves and masters alike were fellow-servants of one Lord, Jesus Christ. And in the service of Christ—in the church fellowship, for example—a Christian slave might be recognized as a leader and teacher because of his spiritual gifts and attainment, and receive due deference from his Christian master. But the Christian slave would not on that account render his master less obedience or serve him less faithfully; his obedience and faithfulness would be all the greater because of their spiritual relationship. If the Christian slave had an unbelieving master, he would serve him the more faithfully now because the honour of Christ and the gospel was bound up with the quality of his service. It might very well be that the fact of his Christian profession would expose him to greater exploitation and persecution at the hands of his pagan master or fellow-slaves; but the sense of Christ's approval would be his prized recompense.

with fear and trembling,—Not with servile fear of his master, but with the fear of God in his heart. The collocation of 'fear and trembling' in the service of God appears in 1 Cor. 2. 3 with reference to Paul himself and in 2 Cor. 7. 15 and Phil. 2. 12 with reference to Christians. For Christian slaves the service of their earthly masters was a special form of the service of God, to be discharged in a spirit of reverence towards Him. They were not to tremble lest anything unpleasant might happen to themselves, but lest their Lord's name should be brought into disrepute through them.

in singleness of your heart, as unto Christ;—Let them do their appointed work honestly, *for Christ's sake.*

> All may of thee partake;
> Nothing can be so mean,
> Which with this tincture, 'for thy sake',
> Will not grow bright and clean.
> A servant with this clause
> Makes drudgery divine;
> Who sweeps a room, as for thy laws,
> Makes that and the action fine.[1]

V. 6 not in the way of eyeservice, as men-pleasers; but as servants of Christ, doing the will of God from the heart; —Any slave would put on a show of working hard when the master's eye, or the foreman's, was on him. But why should he exert himself except when it was to his advantage to do so? He owed his owner nothing; he was enslaved against his will. Much more blame attaches to the modern clock-watcher, who has freely entered into a contract with his employer and receives an agreed remuneration for his services. But a Christian slave

---

[1] From G. Herbert, *The Elixir.*

in the first century (and much more a Christian employee in the twentieth) has the highest possible motive for doing his work well; it is primarily Christ, and not his earthly master, that he is endeavouring to please. A Christian is Christ's bondslave, and therefore he will do God's will with heart and soul, not as a burden but as a delight.

V. 7 **with good will doing service, as unto the Lord, and not unto men**:—Whereas 'from the heart' (*ek psychēs*) is the reverse of listlessness, 'with good will' (*meta eunoias*) suggests a ready willingness, 'which does not wait to be compelled' (J. A. Robinson).

V. 8 **knowing that whatsoever good thing each one doeth, the same shall he receive again from the Lord, whether** *he be* **bond or free.**—It is Christ, and not one's earthly master, who is the final arbiter and rewarder of work well done. This would encourage a Christian slave to work cheerfully and zestfully even for a master who was unreasonable in his demands and impossible to please; he knew that it was from Christ that his thanks would come. The 'receiving again' might no doubt be experienced in measure in the present life (the consciousness of Christ's commendation is a most satisfying reward), but ultimately it is the judgement-seat of Christ that the apostle has in view, where His decisive 'Well done' will be pronounced. The converse truth is emphasized in Col. 3. 25: 'For he that doeth wrong shall receive again the wrong that he hath done; and there is no respect of persons' (R.V. margin).

V. 9 **And, ye masters, do the same things unto them, and forbear threatening: knowing that both their Master and yours is in heaven, and there is no respect of persons with him.**—Masters like Philemon had their obligations, as had slaves like Onesimus. Onesimus's heavenly Master is Philemon's Master as well, and Philemon is responsible to Him for his treatment of Onesimus. The Christian master therefore must not adopt a hectoring or browbeating attitude towards his slaves, but treat them fairly, rendering to them 'that which is just and equal' (Col. 4. 1). The Lord is impartial in His assessments, but more is required from those to whom more is given.

No command is given for the manumission of slaves. In the Epistle to Philemon, indeed, Philemon is given a broad hint of what is expected of him personally in this regard, but at the same time it is made clear that the virtue of such an action would lie precisely in its being done 'not . . . as of necessity, but of free will' (Philem. 14). But to counsel the emancipation of slaves on a general scale would have been to confirm the suspicion of many people in authority that the gospel aimed at the subversion of society. It was better to state the principles of the gospel clearly, and leave them to have their own effect in due course on this iniquitous institution. The slave was legally a member of the master's household or family, and if a Christian master took seriously Paul's injunction to masters, his slaves would be members of his family in more than a merely legal sense, and have more real protection than they might have if manumitted. But slavery under the best conditions is slavery none the less, and it could not survive where the gospel had free course.

No doubt critical situations could arise between Christian masters and slaves for which no detailed prescription could be found in Paul's exhortation to both. But the basic and abiding Christian principles are there, so firmly rooted in the eternal gospel that they can be applied in all changing social structures, and speak to the condition of many today as they did when first they were written.

6. The Panoply of God (6. 10-20)

V. 10 Finally, be strong in the Lord, and in the strength of his might.—An exhortation to spiritual strength is common in the New Testament; we may compare 1 Cor. 16. 13, where 'be strong' represents Gk. *krataioomai*, and 2 Tim. 2. 1, where 'be strengthened' (R.V.) renders Gk. *endynamoomai*, the same verb as is used here (it is used of Paul in Acts 9. 22, and Paul uses it in the active voice with reference to God as his strengthener or enabler in Phil. 4. 13; 1 Tim. 1. 12; 2 Tim. 4. 17). Earlier in this epistle (3. 16) Paul has prayed that his readers might 'be strengthened (Gk. *krataioomai*) with power (Gk. *dynamis*) through his spirit in the inward man', and here again he makes it plain that the Christian's spiritual strength must be a sharing in the power of God as He imparts it to His people. Col. 1. 11 is a noteworthy parallel. The phrase 'in the strength (Gk. *kratos*) of his might' (Gk. *ischys*) is probably to be regarded as a Hebraic genitive construction, meaning 'in his mighty strength', as previously in Eph. 1. 19, where the reference is to the power of God exerted in the raising of Christ. It is that same resurrection power that is put at the believer's disposal.

V. 11 **Put on the whole armour of God,**—The spiritual equipment which is necessary for the Christian's strengthening is described in detail under the figure of various pieces of armour, defensive and offensive. Something like this appears in an earlier epistle of Paul's, where he encourages the Thessalonian Christians to 'be sober, putting on the breastplate of faith and love; and for a helmet, the hope of salvation' (1 Thess. 5. 8). Here the figure is developed more elaborately, as he mentions one by one the parts which make up the divine panoply (the Greek word which he uses is *panoplia*, here rendered 'whole armour'). It is difficult to think of any element in the Christian's spiritual equipment which is not included under one head or another in the following sentences. One writer, indeed, the Puritan William Gurnall, so expounded Eph. 6. 10-17 in his massive work, *The Christian in Complete Armour* (1655), as to make his exposition an exhaustive body of practical divinity.

It has been suggested that Paul goes into greater detail here than elsewhere in listing one by one the pieces of the Christian's armour because he had an object-lesson constantly with him in the person of the Roman soldier who guarded him. However that may be, he frequently speaks of Christian life and service in military terms. These are specially common in the Pastoral Epistles, where, for example, Timothy is exhorted to suffer hardship with Paul 'as a good soldier of Christ Jesus' (2 Tim. 2. 3) and to 'fight the good fight of the faith' like the apostle himself (1 Tim. 6. 12; 2 Tim. 4. 7). But in the earlier letters, too, Paul regards his apostolic labours as so many campaigns in which he fights with spiritual weapons and storms spiritual strongholds (2 Cor. 10. 4); his colleagues are fellow-soldiers (Phil. 2. 25; Philem. 2) and those who share his captivity are fellow-prisoners-of-war (Rom. 16. 7; Col. 4. 10; Philem. 23).

that ye may be able to stand against the wiles of the devil.—As when he warned his readers against 'the wiles of error' (Eph. 4. 14) he had in mind deceptive stratagems by which the truth of the gospel was liable to be perverted, so here (using the same Greek word *methodia*) he refers to the stratagems by which the supreme enemy endeavours to gain an advantage over the people of God in their spiritual warfare. Paul himself had had abundant experience of those stratagems: Satan could put obstacles in the way of his apostolic service (1 Thess. 2. 18), could exploit the most intimate human relationships to the detriment of Christian testimony (1 Cor. 7. 5), could take the form of an angel of light so as to lead believers astray from the true path of simplicity and purity (2 Cor. 11. 3, 14). Well might the apostle say: 'we are not ignorant of his devices' (2 Cor. 2. 11). But if his devices are to be detected and frustrated, heavenly strength is necessary.

V. 12 **For our wrestling is not against flesh and blood, but against the principalities, against the powers,**—For wrestling or fighting on the human plane, human strength will suffice. But it is not on the human plane that the Christian warfare is fought out, but in the spiritual realm, and in that realm only spiritual resources can avail. In himself the Christian is incapable of gaining the mastery over the principalities and powers that would fain bring him into bondage; only the power of Christ can help him. A general reference to principalities and powers has already been made in Eph. 1. 21 and 3. 10; more about them may be learned from the companion Epistle to the Colossians. They rank among the highest angel-princes in the hierarchy of the heavenly places, yet all of them owe their existence to Christ, through whom they were created (Col. 1. 16), and who is accordingly 'the head of all principality and power' (Col. 2. 10).

But some at least of these principalities and powers have embarked upon rebellion against God and not only seek to force men to pay them the worship that is due to Him, but launched an assault upon the crucified Christ at a time when they thought they had Him at their mercy. But He, far from suffering their assault without resistance, grappled with them and overcame them, stripping them of their armour and driving them before Him in His triumphal procession (Col. 2. 15).[1] Thus the hostile powers of evil which Christians must encounter are already vanquished powers, but it is only through faith-union with the victorious Christ that Christians can make His triumph theirs.

against the world-rulers of this darkness, against the spiritual *hosts* **of wickedness in the heavenly** *places*.—These 'world-rulers' (Gk. *kosmokratores*) played a considerable part in the thinking of many in apostolic times. By some (for example, the heretical teachers who were urging their views on the Colossian Christians) they were evidently identified with the lords of the seven planetary spheres, who were believed to dominate the fortunes of men and nations. But a more biblical understanding of them may be obtained from a study of the book of Daniel, where the affairs of the Persian and Greek Empires are seen to be controlled by two angel-princes, who impede, although they cannot ultimately prevent, the execution of divine commissions in the upper world (Dan. 10. 13, 20). Each of these princes might well be called a *kosmokratōr*. The leader of these hostile powers is referred to by Paul in 2 Cor. 4. 4 as 'the god of this age', who has blinded the minds of unbelievers to the light of the gospel.[2] The present world-order as organized in rebellion against God remains under the domination of these powers; only in Christ can men gain the victory over them and be released from their grasp (cf. 1 John 5. 19). The appearance of Christ on earth was the signal for an unprecedented outburst of activity on the part of the realm of darkness controlled by these world-rulers, as though they knew that a mortal threat was being presented to

---

[1] Cf. Eph. 4. 8 and accompanying exposition (pp. 81 ff.).
[2] Cf. Eph. 2. 2, with accompanying exposition (p. 48).

their dominion. And indeed His coming sealed their doom, although, during the present overlapping of the new age and the old, they continue to exercise control over those who have not availed themselves of the way of release. Against such 'spiritual hosts of wickedness in the heavenly places' the Christian must be equipped with the panoply of God if he is to withstand them successfully.

V. 13 **Wherefore take up the whole armour of God, that ye may be able to withstand in the evil day, and, having done all, to stand.**—'The evil day' is the present age; compare Eph. 5. 16, 'the days are evil'. The age is evil because of the evil forces which, although vanquished by Christ, are still able to exercise control over a world which will not avail itself of the fruits of Christ's victory. The truth of the apostolic teaching on this subject is apparent to the clear-sighted observer of the world of the mid-twentieth century. Modern man may not think in terms of principalities and powers, and may consider himself emancipated from outmoded beliefs in angels and demons. But he is all too conscious of powerful and malignant forces operating against him, which he will not hesitate to describe as demonic. He knows that his individual strength is insufficient to resist them, and he is not at all sure that even united action will be more effective. These forces may be Frankenstein monsters of his own creation which no longer obey his commands; they may be subliminal horrors beyond his conscious control. He feels himself to be a helpless victim in a hostile cosmic order which is carrying him to destruction which he cannot avert. He knows himself to be involved in situations against which his moral sense revolts, but he cannot do anything effective about it. He fears that he may be little more than a puppet in the hands of a blind and un-pitying fate, and that it matters little whether he resists and is crushed at once, or acquiesces and is crushed later. There is only one message that can bring hope to such a mood of frustra-tion and despair, and that is the liberating message of the gospel. Christ has won the victory, and those who place their faith in Him may win the victory, too—and know these forces, for all

9

their malignity, to be beaten forces. 'This is the victory that
hath overcome the world, even our faith' (1 John 5. 4). But
even so, so determined is the opposition which these forces offer
to the believer that only by taking the armour of God and putting
forth all his exertions can he hope to stand his ground against
them.

V. 14 **Stand therefore, having girded your loins with
truth, and having put on the breastplate of righteousness,**
—The various pieces of defensive armour recommended to the
believer are the Christian graces which are elsewhere described
as 'the fruit of the Spirit' (Gal. 5. 22 f.). Truth is to be his girdle
and righteousness his breastplate. Truth includes loyalty and
faithfulness; the coming Messiah wears the girdle of faithfulness
(LXX 'truth') in Isa. 11. 5. Righteousness is righteousness of
character and practice here, rather than the believer's righteous
status in the sight of God; in Isa. 59. 17 God Himself is pictured
as putting on 'righteousness as a breastplate, and an helmet of
salvation upon his head' (cf. Eph. 6. 17). John Bunyan notes
that the armour with which Christian was fitted out in the House
Beautiful included no protection for his back, so that in his encounter with Apollyon he could not turn back, but had to stand
and face the foe.

V. 15 **and having shod your feet with the preparation of
the gospel of peace**;—Here, too, we can discern an Isaianic
background: 'How beautiful upon the mountains are the feet of
him that bringeth good tidings, that publisheth peace' (Isa. 52. 7).[1]
Every Christian should be a bearer of God's good news, and a ready
activity in the discharge of this responsibility will be for his own
spiritual well-being as well as for the blessing of others.

V. 16 **withal taking up the shield of faith, wherewith ye
shall be able to quench all the fiery darts of the evil** *one*.—
Alongside 'withal' (Gk. *en pasin*, lit. 'in all') there is a variant
reading 'in addition to all' (Gk. *epi pasin*), reflected in A.V. and
R.S.V. 'above all'. The shield envisaged here (Gk. *thyreos*) is

---

[1] Cf. Eph. 2. 17 (p. 55).

the large body-shield (Latin *scutum*), not the smaller circular shield used by the Greeks (Gk. *aspis*). Faith in God is a comprehensive protection against the flaming shafts of evil which are aimed at the souls of the people of God. Darts and similar missiles were dipped in pitch or some other combustible material, which was then set alight so that the missiles, when released, might serve the purpose of the incendiary bombs of our own day. But Satan's darts, says Paul, are not only stopped but extinguished when met by resolute faith. So one of the subtlest of our Lord's temptations, the temptation to put God to the test by placing Himself in a position where only divine intervention could save Him from death, spent itself ineffectively when met by a faith in His heavenly Father which required no outward sign to assure Him that He was indeed His beloved Son.

V. 17 **And take the helmet of salvation,**—So Paul had previously exhorted the Thessalonian Christians to put on 'for a helmet, the hope of salvation' (1 Thess. 5. 8), echoing the language of Isa. 59. 17, quoted above.

and the sword of the Spirit, which is the word of God: —The 'word' (Gk. *rhēma*, as in Eph. 5. 26) is that utterance of God appropriate to the occasion which the Spirit, so to speak, puts into the believer's hand to be wielded as a sword which will put his spiritual assailants to flight. Our Lord's threefold use of this sword when tempted in the wilderness may serve as an example and encouragement to all His followers. This is the one weapon of attack in the panoply of God; against it there is no defence, 'for the word (*logos*) of God is living, and active, and sharper than any two-edged sword' (Heb. 4. 12). In the Old Testament God speaks of slaying His disobedient people by the words of His mouth (Hos. 6. 5), and of the Messiah it is prophesied that 'he shall smite the earth with the rod of his mouth, and with the breath[1] of his lips shall he slay the wicked' (Isa. 11. 4). So when John in the Revelation sees the Conqueror whose name is called 'The Word of God', the sharp sword which pro-

---

[1] LXX *pneuma*, the word translated 'Spirit' in Eph. 6. 17

ceeds from His mouth for the smiting of the nations is that same powerful utterance which speaks with all the authority of heaven (Rev. 19. 13, 15). No word of man is capable of routing the spiritual hosts of wickedness, but they cannot stand their ground when God speaks.

> And let the prince of ill
> Look grim as e'er he will,
> He harms us not a whit,
> For why his doom is writ;
> A word shall quickly slay him (*Luther*).

V. 18 **with all prayer and supplication praying at all seasons in the Spirit,**—Paul now passes from metaphor to the literal language of the spiritual conflict. When Christian receives his armour in *The Pilgrim's Progress* the weapon of 'All-prayer' is given as one which will stand him in good stead when everything else fails, and with this he prevails against the fiends which beset him in the Valley of the Shadow: when he poured out his soul in fervent prayer 'they gave back, and came no farther'. 'Prayer and supplication'—*proseuchē* and *deēsis*[1] —cannot be sharply distinguished, but their conjunction adds intensity to the apostle's words. Like his Lord, he urges that men 'ought always to pray, and not to faint' (Luke 18. 1); but prayer, to be effective, must be prayer inwrought by the Holy Spirit. (In 1 Cor. 14. 15 'I will pray with the spirit' has probably a different force; the 'spirit' there appears from the context to be the apostle's own spirit, as the 'understanding' in the following clause, 'and I will pray with the understanding also', is his own understanding.)

and watching thereunto in all perseverance and supplication for all the saints,—Their prayers should be offered 'both for themselves and those who call them friend' (Tennyson). The bond of fellowship which unites the people of God is never more effective than when they are praying for one another. Persistence in prayer is enjoined, and also watchfulness, spiritual

---

[1] In so far as they are distinguishable, *proseuchē* is the more general word for 'prayer 'while *deēsis* means 'request' or 'entreaty'.

alertness, lest they be overtaken unawares by some spiritual enemy. Several times the exhortation to watch and pray recurs in the New Testament, most notably in our Lord's warning to His disciples in the garden of Gethsemane: 'watch and pray, that ye enter not into temptation' (Mark 14. 38). Two words are translated 'watch' in such contexts—*agrypneō* (as here) and *grēgoreō*—but both have the same basic sense of keeping awake.

V. 19 **and on my behalf, that utterance may be given unto me in opening my mouth, to make known with boldness the mystery of the gospel,**—It is possible, as R.V. margin points out, to take 'with boldness' (Gk. *en parrhēsia*, 'with full freedom of speech')[1] with 'opening my mouth' instead of with 'to make known'; R.V. text gives the more probable punctuation, but it makes little practical difference either way. Paul, living under house-arrest in Rome, felt his need of his friends' prayers— not so much for his own well-being as for the cause of the gospel to which his life was completely devoted. So, in the companion-letter, he asks the Colossian Christians to pray 'that God may open unto us a door for the word, to speak the mystery of Christ, for which I am also in bonds; that I may make it manifest, as I ought to speak' (Col. 4. 3 f.). Some authorities, possibly includ-ing the oldest of all, papyrus 46, omit 'of the gospel'; but the preponderant evidence favours its retention. In any case, the mystery here *is* the gospel—'the mystery which hath been kept in silence through times eternal, but now is manifested, and by the scriptures of the prophets, according to the commandment of the eternal God, is made known unto all the nations for the obedience of faith' (Rom. 16. 25 f.).

V. 20 **for which I am an ambassador in chains**;—Strictly, as R.V. margin points out, 'in a chain'; that is, the chain (Gk. *halysis*) around his wrist by which he was handcuffed to the soldier who guarded him. The soldier would be relieved every four hours or so; but there was no relief from his chain for Paul, only a change of soldier. Many people have wondered from

---

[1] Cf. Eph. 3. 12 with accompanying exposition (p. 65).

time to time what it must have meant for a Roman soldier to be handcuffed to a man like Paul! A prisoner? Which of the two was the prisoner? Paul thinks of himself as the ambassador of Jesus Christ, duly accredited to represent his Lord at the imperial court of Rome—a chained ambassador, indeed, but an ambassador none the less. 'Because of the hope of Israel I am bound with this chain', he could say to the Jews of Rome (Acts 28. 20), but the hope of Israel was the hope of the Gentiles, too (Rom. 15. 12); and the apostle of the Gentiles wore his chain as a decoration or badge of office, since it had come to him through the exercise of his apostleship.

that in it I may speak boldly, as I ought to speak.—By 'in it' he does not mean the chain, but the gospel revelation; the Chester Beatty papyrus 46 and the Vatican Codex read simply 'it' (*auto*) instead of 'in it' (*en autō*). Paul had no doubt about the message he had to proclaim; it was the one and only gospel. But he was concerned to proclaim it worthily, in the fitting manner; in other words, to proclaim it freely and boldly (*parrhēsiazomai*).[1] To this end he sought his readers' prayers. Were their prayers answered? Let Luke, Paul's companion, bear his testimony: 'he abode two whole years in his own hired dwelling, and received all that went in unto him, preaching the kingdom of God, and teaching the things concerning the Lord Jesus Christ *with all boldness* (*parrhēsia*), none forbidding him' (Acts 28. 20).

7. FINAL GREETINGS (6. 21-24)

V. 21 But that ye also may know my affairs, how I do, Tychicus, the beloved brother and faithful minister in the Lord, shall make known to you all things:—The reference to Tychicus is almost word for word identical with Col. 4. 7 f. He was evidently the bearer of the letter to Colossae as well as of this one, and also possibly of a letter to Laodicea (Col. 4. 16). Onesimus, who went with Tychicus as his travel-companion, is not mentioned here, although it was appropriate to name him

---

[1] The verb is derived from *parrhēsia* ('freedom of speech'), the noun used above in verse 19 (cf. Eph. 3. 12).

in the letter to the Colossian church, to which he belonged, and also, of course, in the letter to Philemon, of which he himself was the bearer. As for Tychicus, he was a native of the province of Asia, as can be learned from Acts 20. 4, where he is included among the delegates of the Gentile churches who accompanied Paul to Judaea in A.D. 57 to hand over those churches' gifts to their brethren in Jerusalem. He is mentioned also in the Pastoral Epistles as a messenger of Paul (2 Tim. 4. 12; Titus 3. 12). On the present occasion he was probably Paul's special envoy to the churches of the province of Asia which had been planted in the course of Paul's Ephesian ministry, to deliver this letter, or copies of it, to all of them. In Col. 4. 7 Paul not only calls him his 'beloved brother and faithful minister' (*diakonos*, 'attendant'), as here, but also his fellow-slave (*syndoulos*).

V. 22 **whom I have sent unto you for this very purpose, that ye may know our state, and that he may comfort your hearts.**—'I have sent' is an example of the 'epistolary aorist'; the writer speaks from the standpoint of his readers. Our idiom requires the present: 'I am sending'. Tychicus will give the Asian Christians all the apostle's news, and strengthen and cheer their hearts.

V. 23 **Peace be to the brethren, and love with faith, from God the Father and the Lord Jesus Christ.**—The more general terms of this verse and the following suggest the circular character of the letter, addressed to 'the brethren, . . . all them that love our Lord Jesus Christ in uncorruptness'. The peace which he bespeaks for them is no conventional salutation, but the enjoyment of the peace which comes 'from God the Father and the Lord Jesus Christ'. From that source, too, comes the love combined with faith which he desires to abound among them. For the conjunction of love and faith we may compare the longer text of Eph. 1. 15 (cf. Col. 1. 4). The close association of God and Christ in such expressions has been commented on in the note on the initial salutation in Eph. 1. 2.

V. 24 **Grace be with all them that love our Lord Jesus Christ in uncorruptness.**—He closes, as he began, with the

invocation of God's grace upon his readers. The R.V. rendering
'in uncorruptness' is literal, but a trifle ungainly; the American
Standard Version (1901) is better: 'Grace be with all them that
love our Lord Jesus Christ with a love incorruptible'. An un-
fading and undying love is meant; 'uncorruptness' (*aphtharsia*)
is practically synonymous with immortality.[1] Where such love
for Christ is present, the grace of God can never be absent.

---

[1] As in 1 Cor. 15. 42, 50, 53, 54; cf. Rom. 2. 7; 2 Tim. 1. 10 (in all of which
R.V. renders it by 'incorruption').

INDEX

INDEX